Hollywood 1900s

Hollywood 1900s

Douglas Jarvis

admiral

This book was devised and produced by
Multimedia Publications (UK) Ltd

Editor: Richard Rosenfeld
Assistant Editor: Dan Millar
Production: Karen Bromley
Design: Mick Hodson
Picture Research: David Sutherland

Copyright © Douglas Jarvis 1986

First published in the United Kingdom, 1986 by Admiral Books an
imprint owned jointly by WH Smith and Son Limited, Registered No
237811, England, trading as WHS Distributors, St John's House,
East Street, Leicester LE1 6NE and Multimedia Publications (UK)
Limited, Central House, 1 Ballards Lane, London N1 1UZ.

ISBN 1851 7104 50

Typeset by Letterspace Limited
Origination by Imago
Printed in Italy by Sagdos, Milan

Contents

Endpapers: *Sue Lyon as **Lolita** in Stanley Kubrick's 1962 version of Vladimir Nabokov's controversial novel.*

Page 1: *Paul McCartney, one of the four Beatles, as seen by Heinz Edelman and his team of artists in **Yellow Submarine** (1968), the first British-made cartoon feature for 14 years. This fascinating compendium of all the art and fashion fads of the day came nearer than most live-action films to explaining the phenomenon of the Sixties.*

Page 2: *Julie Andrews (left) and Mary Tyler Moore as flappers in George Roy Hill's charmingly frothy musical dessert **Thoroughly Modern Milly** (1967), a successful lampoon of a much lampooned era.*

This page: *Audrey Hepburn as Eliza Doolittle in **My Fair Lady** (1964), wearing the famous Edwardian black-and-white Ascot ensemble created by Cecil Beaton in the grand tradition of motion picture costume design.*

Blockbusters

Chapter 1

Everything changed for Hollywood in the Sixties, and Hollywood didn't like it. In its 50-year existence, the American film industry had surmounted two major upheavals. The first of these was the coming of sound in 1927, an innovation resisted by a community not noted for its forward-looking attitudes. Yet the public soon decreed that silent movies were dead, and the talkies eventually proved to be a shot in the arm for the film capital of the world.

The second crisis was the divorce of exhibition from production and distribution. The Hollywood majors believed in their inalienable right not only to distribute the films their studios made but also to show them in their own theaters, but the American government stood firm in its move to break the industry's monopoly. The battle, interrupted by the war, lasted 20 years. But from 1948 to 1959 antitrust laws compelled the major companies to divorce their studios from their cinema chains and cease block-booking; the last major to capitulate was Loew's/MGM.

Pessimists predicted that these laws would kill the film industry. Needless to say it survived, and despite the strong threat from television. The threat took two forms. The first struck in January 1960 when the Screen section of the Writers' Guild went on strike for a share of the profits of movies sold by the studios to television. The actors' and directors' organizations followed suit. The second – that television kept potential audiences at home – was rejected by the industry, which argued that audiences were still flocking to the movies, not least to see 1959's big hit, **Ben-Hur**.

This epic was shot, of course, in one of the wide-screen processes considered to be the answer to any threat from television. The most ambitious process was Cinerama, but by 1960 the novelty had worn off: Cinerama's cameras had filmed most of the world's natural wonders and were now running out of places to show on the giant wrap-around screen. Audiences too were tiring of these travelogues (as well as the inevitable flickering between the three projected images). Cinerama executives believed that the rot could be stopped if they combined spectacle with a story and, thinking back to the kind of profits earned by **Around the World in 80 Days** (1956) they signed an agreement with MGM to cooperate on **How the West Was Won** (1962).

The big screen

Winning the West gave opportunities for an all-star cast – including John Wayne, Gregory Peck, James Stewart, Henry Fonda, Richard

*The climactic scene from **The Greatest Story Ever Told** (1965).*

Widmark, Debbie Reynolds and Robert Preston – to shoot the rapids, fight, and indulge in train and horse chases. Audiences approved, though few were inclined to experience **The Wonderful World of the Brothers Grimm** (1962), a second cooperation between the two companies which proved that Cinerama in itself was no attraction. Nor was its less than all-star cast, including Laurence Harvey, Claire Bloom and Karl Boehm.

But there were 20 comic talents, plus Spencer Tracy, in **It's a Mad, Mad, Mad, Mad World** (1963), which, with one screen and one projector, had the added attraction of eliminating those maddening wobbly lines, and was supposed to make the audience take Cinerama to their hearts once again. A three-hour knockabout comedy concerning a search for buried treasure over much of California and Nevada, the film was produced and directed for United Artists by Stanley Kramer, who could not resist the sort of message conveyed in his more serious films – this one, naturally, underlining the evils of greed.

Cinerama was saved, and United Artists gathered yet another all-star cast, including Charlton Heston, Sidney Poitier, Pat Boone and Dorothy McGuire, for a Cinerama version of Fulton Oursler's best-selling interpretation of the life of Christ, **The Greatest Story Ever Told** (1965), directed by the much-respected George Stevens. Christ was played by Max von Sydow, the superb Swedish actor known from his work in Ingmar Bergman's films, and even John Wayne showed up for one line: "This truly was the son of God."

The film seemed likely to be a big box-office success. **Ben-Hur** had reaffirmed the popularity of the religious spectacle and had brought fresh laurels to the veteran director William Wyler, who had accepted the challenge of breathing new life into an old tale. Stevens, like Wyler, belonged to that group of film-makers admired by critics and able to win Oscars, which was why they had achieved a degree of independence; the studio moguls were not too happy about this, but were forced to agree that these were the talents most likely to bring them prestige and respectable financial returns.

The Greatest Story Ever Told, however, was not a studio project but one of Stevens' own; 20th Century-Fox turned it down as costs mounted, but United Artists was happy to be associated with a director who had received acclaim in the Fifties for **A Place in the Sun** (1951), **Shane** (1953) and **Giant** (1956). That acclaim was not forthcoming on this occasion. The much-vaunted all-star casts of **How the West Was Won** and **It's a Mad, Mad, Mad, Mad World** had enabled both to sell tickets despite poor notices, but when the public spurned **The Greatest Story Ever Told**, Cinerama was doomed. The film, much cut, played most of its engagements in a CinemaScope print. CinemaScope was also doomed, but that was only because its place was taken by an identical but much cheaper anamorphic wide-screen process, 35mm Panavision.

Below left: *Some of the cast of thousands welcome Christ into Jerusalem in* **The Greatest Story Every Told** *(1965).*

Bottom: *A spectacular scene from the multi-million dollar Technirama 70 Roman epic* **Spartacus** *(1960) with Kirk Douglas (center) in the title role. Also in the all-star cast were Laurence Olivier, Jean Simmons, Tony Curtis, Charles Laughton and Peter Ustinov.*

Below: *Kirk Douglas (foreground) as* **Spartacus** *brandishes a stave as he leads the revolt of the slaves (among them John Ireland and Harold J. Stone just behind him) in the Ancient Rome of 73 BC, as imagined by director Stanley Kubrick.*

The wider screens, especially when enhanced with color and stereophonic sound, had revitalized cinemagoing during the Fifties. The small black-and-white screen at home couldn't compete with movies which were clearly events, and which had temporarily revived the old concept of "roadshow exhibition".

Rivaling Broadway

By 1960 the industry was geared to producing a handful of movies — or roadshows — annually which were as much of a night out as a big Broadway show. The public booked ahead at advanced prices for the "event", which was preceded by an overture and was sufficiently lengthy to require a profitable interval. An all-color souvenir book was available for those wishing to relive the magic, while a soundtrack album for a wide range of films, not just musicals, could be bought in record shops.

But the "big night out" treatment didn't always work. John Wayne's **The Alamo** (1960), which he starred in and produced, was his personal statement and account of the famous battle of 1836, which he believed every American would want to see. He couldn't have been more wrong. Instead the public flocked to the Roman epic **Spartacus** (1960). This was also produced by an actor as a vehicle for himself, Kirk Douglas, but whereas Wayne's only big co-star was Richard Widmark, Douglas had the sense to include two top box-office names, Tony Curtis and Jean Simmons, plus Laurence Olivier, Charles Laughton and Peter Ustinov to commend the

Above: *The $750,000 motor-operated reproduction of HMS* Bounty *constructed for* **Mutiny on the Bounty** *(1962) was only part of the $19-million cost of the movie, ten times that of the 1935 version.*

Right: *Marlon Brando (right) put on an English accent for his foppish Fletcher Christian, playing opposite Trevor Howard (left) as Captain Bligh in* **Mutiny on the Bounty**. *While on location in Tahiti, Brando met Tarita, a Tahitian with whom he has two children.*

enterprise to the critics. Moreover, **Spartacus** was entertaining and **The Alamo** wasn't — largely owing to their screenplays and, to a lesser extent, their direction. When no major film-maker had showed interest in making **The Alamo**, Wayne decided to direct it himself, although he hoped until well into the production that the job would be taken over as a favor to him by his friend John Ford, master director of the Western.

Spartacus began with Anthony Mann in the directorial chair but, after a dispute with him, Douglas called upon Hollywood's brightest new talent, Stanley Kubrick. He agreed to tackle the job partly as a return favor to Douglas whose decision to take on the star part in **Paths of Glory** (1957) attracted much needed financial backing.

Star power

Some stars carried a lot of weight in the early Sixties. Throughout Hollywood history, they had snatched at power. The studio tycoons had blenched at the clout attained in the Twenties by Charles Chaplin, Mary Pickford and Douglas Fairbanks, and vowed not to let any such thing happen again. Nor did it until the studio system broke down in the early Fifties.

Left: *'The Rivers' episode from the first fiction film to be presented in Cinerama,* **How the West Was Won** *(1962). Fighting the rapids are Debbie Reynolds (left), Agnes Moorehead (center), Carroll Baker (right) and Karl Malden (background).*

Below: *A scene from the Civil War interlude of* **How the West Was Won***, directed by John Ford and featuring his favorite actor John Wayne (left). The other four episodes in this all-star Cinerama Western were directed by two other stalwarts of the genre, Henry Hathaway and George Marshall.*

Above: *Richard Burton (in plumed helmet) as Mark Antony fights to save his war galley from being taken over by Octavian's legionaries in Joseph L. Mankiewicz's* **Cleopatra**, *the picture that almost bankrupted 20th Century-Fox.*

Above right: *The $37-million* **Cleopatra** *(1963) was described as being 'conceived in a state of emergency, shot in confusion and winding up in blind panic'. It did, however, provide gossip columnists with copy on the off-screen love affair between Elizabeth Taylor (center) as the Queen of Egypt and Richard Burton.*

Right: *'She makes hungry where most she satisfies.'*

One of the surviving moguls, Darryl F. Zanuck, publicly criticized John Wayne for taking unto himself the powers of producer and director, but it was a naive statement. Although their names only appeared on the cast lists, some stars controlled every aspect of their vehicles – and in the early Sixties these included Charlton Heston, William Holden, Gregory Peck, Frank Sinatra, Burt Lancaster and Cary Grant, the only one of the pre-war stars who was also in all but name his own producer.

Anthony Quinn and Paul Newman soon acquired the same degree of autonomy; Yul Brynner held it briefly, as did Glenn Ford, until it was taken from both because of box-office failures – in Ford's case after two expensive remakes of old Hollywood favorites, **Cimarron** (1960) and **The Four Horsemen of the Apocalypse** (1962). In between these two, Ford appeared in another remake, **Pocketful of Miracles** (1961), Frank Capra's revised version of his own **Lady for a Day** (1933). Incidentally, Capra's autobiography, *The Name Above the Title*, contains an eloquent account of Ford's whims and tantrums when he subjected the great veteran director to constant humiliations. After similar experiences with John Wayne's advisers, when he was preparing to direct Wayne in **Circus World** (1964), Capra decided to leave the industry he had served so magnificently.

Among the most powerful stars was Marlon Brando, acknowledged as both a superb actor and a box-office favorite. All his projects received wide press coverage, and with this in mind Paramount gave him total control on **One-Eyed Jacks** (1961), as

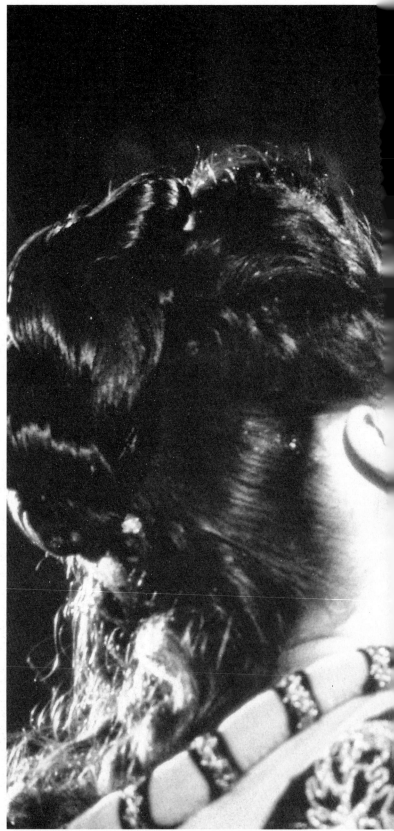

well as all profits after the cost had been recouped. Not long after shooting began, Brando began to fall out with the director, Stanley Kubrick, who subsequently left the film. Brando took over as director and acquitted himself so honorably on this harsh Western that it is a pity that he hasn't accepted that responsibility since.

Search for the blockbuster

Subsequently Brando wielded even greater power at MGM. Several times in its history MGM's fortunes had been restored by pouring its resources into one costly film — as with the silent **Ben-Hur** (1926), a cogent consideration when they contemplated the 1959 remake. Receipts from that remake and a reissue of **Gone With the Wind** convinced executives that they needed another blockbuster, one with reissue potential if times got tough. They decided that the old MGM success most demanding a new treatment was **Mutiny on the Bounty** (1935), about a half-forgotten incident in British naval history.

Asked to play the evil Captain Bligh in the 1962 version, Brando refused, but added that he might be interested in playing Fletcher Christian, the leader of the mutineers. The opportunity of getting Brando sent MGM's executives into delirium — in the end the star walked away with an unprecedented $1¼ million, which included bonuses when the film went over schedule (on account of delays for which he himself was often responsible). Brando had been given complete control over production, which may be why Britain's respected Carol Reed was replaced as director by the veteran Russian-American Lewis Milestone, although in the event Milestone loathed working with Brando. The cost of the film escalated to an astounding $19 million, but with final North American rental takings of less than $10 million, Brando could not claim the share of the profits agreed in his contract. It was 18 years before he worked for MGM again.

Simultaneously, 20th Century-Fox was committed to paying a vast

Right: *The marriage of the heroic medieval knight known as **El Cid** to his beloved Chimène (Charlton Heston and Sophia Loren, illustrated). Anthony Mann's 1961 spectacle, shot in Spain, towers above others of the same type.*

salary to Elizabeth Taylor for **Cleopatra** (1963); announced as $1 million by the publicity department, it was, in fact, somewhat less, but large sums were guaranteed if shooting went over schedule. It was not her fault that production in London was shut down and restarted in Rome, with Richard Burton and Rex Harrison respectively replacing Stephen Boyd and Peter Finch, and with a new director, Joseph L. Mankiewicz, who was compelled to rewrite the script as filming progressed.

As costs mounted to $36 million, the studio called for its lawyers, and among the many suits flying about was one accusing Taylor and Burton – enjoying a much-publicized affair – of moral conduct likely to alienate the public. Few of those who eventually saw the film felt that the events on screen were as dramatic as those in the journalists' version of "real life". Apart from Mankiewicz, the only major figure to emerge from the fiasco with credit was Harrison, who played Julius Caesar; critics found Burton monotonous as Mark Antony and Taylor inadequate in the title-role. The critics put forward no pressing reason for seeing the film, and many for avoiding it; though it was easily the top box-office hit of the year and eventually took $26 million in domestic rentals alone, there was no question of this hugely expensive movie recovering its costs in the short run favored by movie accounting, though US and worldwide TV and video income may eventually have soaked up most of the red ink.

Burton and Taylor recovered from this setback to their careers by appearing quickly and quietly in a British movie, **The VIPs** (1963), which enjoyed moderate popularity. Brando behaved similarly (by making the medium-budgeted **The Ugly American**, 1963), so silencing those who wanted him and Taylor thrown out of Hollywood. The truth was that no one individual was responsible for those spiraling budgets. Those to blame were the executives who had allowed these players such power and had then turned a blind eye to the circumstances in which they wielded it.

The blockbuster mentality was revitalized by **Lawrence of Arabia** (1962), produced by Sam Spiegel, who had established a substantial

Above: *Omar Sharif made a sensational debut in English-speaking films (he had previously made Egyptian and French pictures) as Sherif Ali in David Lean's intelligent, brilliantly photographed desert epic,* **Lawrence of Arabia** *(1962).*

Above: *David Lean's* **Lawrence of Arabia** *(1962) – the first of three epics using a Robert Bolt screenplay – attempted some psychological insight into the complex character of T.E. Lawrence as portrayed by Peter O'Toole (with Anthony Quinn, right).*

Right: *Lawrence of Arabia* (1962) alias Peter O'Toole (in white Arab dress) gazes mystically into the beyond as he leads his Bedouin army against the Turks with Omar Sharif, as his friend Sherif Ali ibn el Kharish, by his side.

reputation with such films as **The African Queen** (1951), **On the Waterfront** (1954) and **The Bridge on the River Kwai** (1957). The last-named had been directed by Britain's David Lean, and the two teamed up again for an epic biographical study of the enigmatic Arabist, soldier and writer T.E. Lawrence.

Lawrence of Arabia provided many opportunities for action, spectacular desert photography and a big role (turned down by Brando) for the then relatively unknown Peter O'Toole and almost equally fine parts for newcomer Omar Sharif, Anthony Quinn, Alec Guinness, José Ferrer, Claude Rains and Anthony Quayle. While avoiding any suggestions of homosexuality or masochism, it also intimated that Lawrence was a poseur and discreetly hinted that he had been sexually assaulted while in a Turkish jail, two reasons why the film was regarded as "the thinking man's epic". This was the first film in the history of the cinema which presented a hero in this ambivalent way.

Reliving the past

In the Sixties there was a fascination with films about historical characters, in keeping with the cinema's yearning for intellectual respectability. Charlton Heston, who had been John the Baptist in **The Greatest Story Ever Told**, also played the painter Michelangelo in **The Agony and the Ecstasy** (1965), the title-role of the semi-legendary Spanish warrior in **El Cid** (1961), and the Victorian General Gordon in **Khartoum** (1966), all of which were roadshown. The producer of **El Cid** was Samuel Bronston, who tried to build a career out of epics.

In the Fifties, the American film industry discovered not only that Britain and Italy possessed first-class production facilities, but that filming there was cheaper than at home. Moreover, the pool of talent available in Britain was more suitable to historic tales because of the more "starchy" accent considered essential, and was cheaper to transport to, say, Italy than having a cast brought over from

Above: *A typical 'cast of thousands' scene from Anthony Mann's* **The Fall of the Roman Empire** *(1964), shot at Samuel Bronston's studio in Spain. The same year, Bronston's empire fell when he was forced to suspend production because of heavy debts.*

Right: **The Fall of the Roman Empire** *had its longueurs, but it also contained stunning visuals, an impeccable performance from Alec Guinness as Marcus Aurelius, and the beautiful Sophia Loren (illustrated) as his daughter.*

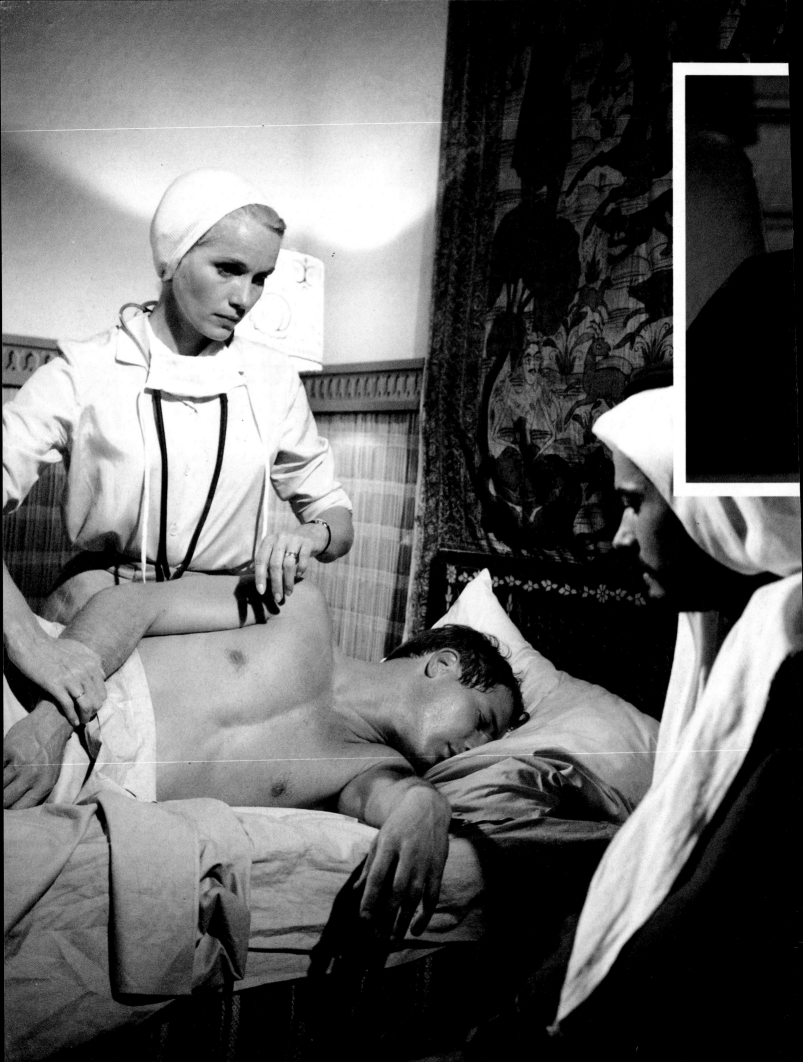

Hollywood. Bronston homed in on Spain and imported supporting players from Britain; while Spanish studios left much to be desired, their personnel came cheap. It was therefore possible to assemble "casts of thousands" by using non-unionized extras at minimal rates. Bronston started with Nicholas Ray's **King of Kings** (1961), a life of Christ, and followed it with Anthony Mann's **El Cid**, Ray's **55 Days at Peking** (1963), a tale of the Boxer Rebellion starring Heston again, Ava Gardner and David Niven, and Mann's **The Fall of the Roman Empire** (1964), with a cast headed by Sophia Loren, James Mason and Alec Guinness. Nicholas Ray and Anthony Mann were skilled commercial film-makers who, much admired by French intellectuals, were later critically acclaimed.

El Cid and **The Fall of the Roman Empire** had particularly impressive visuals, but audiences were less interested in the Boxers battling against the International Settlement in Peking or the Visigoths at the gates of a Roman outpost than heroes like Jesus and the Cid. Bronston, in fact, was helping audiences to kick the blockbuster habit. Roadshow plans were abandoned for his next film, **Circus World** (1964), and takings were not enough to shore up the tottering Bronston empire, which now included a vast new studio complex near Madrid. Bronston's debts were a clear warning: size was not enough.

Yet once again the roadshow concept received a fillip from another spectacle made in Spain, **Doctor Zhivago** (1965), produced by Carlo Ponti, who with his former colleague Dino De Laurentiis had pioneered the international super-production in the Fifties. Both producers had since left Italy for Hollywood and gone their separate

Above center: *Spencer Tracy as the American judge at the* ***Judgment at Nuremberg*** *(1961) listens intently as 'star' witnesses such as Judy Garland, Montgomery Clift and Marlene Dietrich give evidence in Stanley Kramer's well-meaning drama.*

Left: *American nurse Eva Marie Saint attends to wounded resistance leader Paul Newman while his Arab friend John Derek looks on anxiously in Otto Preminger's mammoth 220-minute* ***Exodus*** *(1960).*

Above: *Katharine Hepburn gained the second of her four Oscars for* ***Guess Who's Coming to Dinner*** *(1967), the last of the nine movies she made with her beloved Spencer Tracy.*

ways, but each maintained his interest in blockbusters, and Ponti decided that Boris Pasternak's epic novel of the Russian Revolution was ripe for such treatment. Fresh from their triumph with **Lawrence of Arabia**, David Lean and Robert Bolt were brought in to direct and write, while the title-role was given to Omar Sharif, whose performance in **Lawrence** had made him an international star. **Doctor Zhivago** also featured Julie Christie, Ralph Richardson, Rod Steiger and Alec Guinness. The result was lashings of prestige and five Oscars.

The more serious among the other big movies of the time had mixed receptions. **Judgment at Nuremberg** (1961) was produced and directed by Stanley Kramer, who assembled a cast including Spencer Tracy as the judge, Burt Lancaster as one of the accused Nazis, Maximilian Schell and Richard Widmark for and against the defense, Marlene Dietrich as spokesperson for the good Germans and, in cameo roles, Judy Garland and Montgomery Clift as Nazi victims. **Exodus** (1960), Otto Preminger's film on the founding of the state of Israel, also required an all-star cast: Paul Newman, Eva Marie Saint and Lee J. Cobb. Like Kramer, Otto Preminger was drawn to challenging subjects, especially when based on controversial best-sellers or Broadway hits — in this case Leon Uris's massive Zionist novel.

Both Kramer and Preminger had established their reputations in the Fifties, when their work was praised by the influential critic of the *New York Times*, Bosley Crowther. Individually, they had hits in the Sixties, Preminger with **Advise and Consent** (1962) and Kramer

Left: *One of the many visually impressive scenes from David Lean's 197-minute epic* **Doctor Zhivago** *(1965): the wintry Russian landscape was actually shot in Spain.*

Below: *Omar Sharif as the idealistic Russian doctor-poet in* **Doctor Zhivago** *stares out of his iced-up window with soulful eyes as he dreams of his lost love, Lara.*

with **Guess Who's Coming to Dinner** (1967), and later a run of flops. **Advise and Consent** was based on Allen Drury's political bestseller, and included Henry Fonda, Don Murray, Charles Laughton and Gene Tierney, though the film's strength derived from its narrative rather than its star cast.

Guess Who's Coming to Dinner was based on an original screenplay by William Rose, concerning the reaction of a white couple – played by Spencer Tracy and Katharine Hepburn – to their daughter's impending marriage to a black man – Sidney Poitier.

Columbia released both movies – but roadshowed neither since one was an intimate comedy-drama and the other was a doubtful proposition, for few political films had ever succeeded at the box office. It was also made in black-and-white, as was **Judgment at Nuremberg**, for Hollywood still believed that Technicolor was too frivolous for serious drama. But the black-and-white **The Longest Day** (1962), Darryl F. Zanuck's elaborate all-star reconstruction of the landings in Normandy in 1944, which required the insertion of newsreel material of the period, was roadshowed. It was also Hollywood's last big-budget black-and-white film, as color finally became indispensable during the decade. There were by now many cheaper color systems than Technicolor, and except in the rare instances noted audiences expected color in all major films. After all color was universal in television by the mid-Sixties in the USA and by the end of the decade in the major countries of Europe too.

Left: *The Allied landings in Normandy on June 6, 1944 were the subject of the lengthy (180-minute) Darryl F. Zanuck production **The Longest Day** (1962). A Who's Who of international stars took cameo roles, among them John Wayne (illustrated).*

Above: *The Germans defend the beaches of Normandy in **The Longest Day**. The huge 20th Century-Fox production had three directors, each dealing with their own armies – Ken Annakin (British), Andrew Marton (American) and Bernhard Wicki (German).*

Right: *Washington politicians were put under the microscope in Otto Preminger's all-star **Advise and Consent** (1962). One of them, Don Murray (left foreground), finds himself in a gay bar.*

Musical profits

In the late Thirties when Technicolor was prohibitively expensive except on certain box-office successes, its use had been restricted chiefly to musicals and historical subjects. A musical in black and white was unthinkable by 1950, and for the next few years the combination of song-and-dance and color guaranteed good box-office returns, often for unimaginative versions of Broadway shows.

Chronologically, the first blockbuster of the Sixties was a musical, **Can-Can** (1960). Its producers, 20th Century-Fox, saw no great need to adhere to the original (first staged in 1953), which was not one of Cole Porter's biggest hits, despite having one of his finest scores. That now was cut and supplemented by some of his most hackneyed songs; the material was changed to accommodate

Maurice Chevalier and Louis Jourdan reprising their double-act from **Gigi**, and bowdlerized, curiously, to suit Shirley MacLaine and Frank Sinatra — thus losing its piquancy. The film did not live up to box-office expectations.

MGM, considered the market leader in musicals, meanwhile had only modest successes with **Bells Are Ringing** (1960), in which Judy Holliday repeated her Broadway triumph; **The Unsinkable Molly Brown** (1964), starring Debbie Reynolds; and **Billy Rose's Jumbo** (1962), with Doris Day. Only the last of these was from an *old* (and indeed half-forgotten) Broadway show, but Doris Day, America's favorite female star, was expected to atone for that. Yet the film failed and MGM lost interest in making musicals.

If, however, people were selective in choosing movie musicals, this

Above left: *The bravura high-kicking* **Can-Can**, *the central theme of the 1960 Cole Porter musical of that title. The story of café owner Shirley MacLaine's fight to allow the 'lewd' dance to be performed at her establishment lacked the verve of the title routine.*

Above: *A scene from* **West Side Story** *(1961) which had galvanic dances, exciting music by Leonard Bernstein, and some social consciousness, even if seen in radical-chic showbiz terms. Though the members of the street gangs were meant to be in their teens, the ages of the clean-cut cast ranged from 22 to 30.*

Right: *Natalie Wood and Richard Beymer as Maria and Tony, a contemporary New York Romeo and Juliet, in the most fêted musical film ever, Robert Wise and Jerome Robbins'* **West Side Story**.

Above: *David Tomlinson looks astonished as his son and daughter (Matthew Garber and Karen Dotrice) descend the stairs with their magical governess who arrived by umbrella. Julie Andrews won an Oscar for her remarkable screen debut in* **Mary Poppins** *(1964) in the role of P. L. Travers' nanny.*

Right: *Julie Andrews as* **Mary Poppins** *walks through a Walt Disney cartoon land with her cockney beau Dick Van Dyke.*

was an era in which every Broadway original-cast record album was assured huge sales throughout the country; and indeed, in New York itself the musical had never been healthier. The critics and the public had adored a trailblazing show that switched the story of *Romeo and Juliet* to the contemporary slums of New York, and **West Side Story** (1961) was swiftly brought to the screen by United Artists. They were rewarded with fine notices, a fistful of Oscars and excellent business the world over.

One of the problems of making musicals was that their costs were rising and, because of television, the domestic market was shrinking. This meant a greater dependence on foreign returns, but there were some important foreign markets — notably France — which remained indifferent to the American musical. **West Side Story**, with its electrifying Leonard Bernstein score and direction by Jerome Robbins (who had staged the show on Broadway) and Robert Wise, appeared to signal that there were new audiences for musicals.

Accordingly, Warner Brothers brought **The Music Man** (1962) to the screen, despite its folksy, very American theme. As on Broadway, Morton Da Costa directed and Robert Preston — deemed irreplaceable as the fast-talking traveling salesman who cons a small Iowa

town into starting up a boys' orchestra — played the title role. But the film did poorly in many foreign territories to the extent that Warners' French office didn't bother to open it at all. Preston was not, after all, a big name. And neither was Ethel Merman, which was why Warners did not invite her to repeat her Broadway triumph in **Gypsy** (1962), as the stage-crazy mother of a vaudeville kid (Natalie Wood), whom she turns into a striptease "artist". Although the almost equally raucous Rosalind Russell replaced Merman, Mervyn LeRoy's film lacked the spark of the exhilarating stage original.

My Fair Lady (1964) presented fewer problems for Jack L. Warner, the last of the movie-making brothers, who wanted to finish his career on a high note. With book and lyrics by Alan Jay Lerner and music by Frederick Loewe, this version of Bernard Shaw's *Pygmalion* had been the most acclaimed musical in Broadway history. Its New York run had survived many changes of cast and after eight years was drawing to a close only because its sponsors felt that Warners should start to get a return on the record-breaking $5½ million they paid for the rights — the film couldn't open until the show closed.

Moreover, the show had repeated its Broadway success in every country in which it had been staged – which did not include France, for the impresario who owned the rights hesitated until the film version was upon him. In New York, and subsequently in London, the play had been a triumph for its stars: Rex Harrison as the arrogant Professor Higgins, who teaches a cockney flower girl to speak properly and thereby transforms her into a "lady"; Julie Andrews as Eliza Doolittle and Stanley Holloway as her reprobate father.

Cary Grant was approached to play the Harrison role in the film,

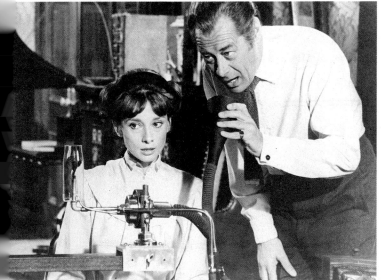

but replied that not only would he not play it, but if Harrison wasn't cast, he wouldn't even go and see it. Warner offered the Holloway role to James Cagney, who refused it; Holloway was the only other possible choice. The beautiful and talented Audrey Hepburn replaced Julie Andrews, who had not then made a movie, and George Cukor, a master-director of civilized art and skilled handler of musical numbers, was asked to make the film. The Warners directive was to reproduce the stage hit.

My Fair Lady, though popular, could not recover its high costs at the box-office, but it might have done better if Julie Andrews had played Eliza, since she was about to become a major star thanks to Walt Disney, who made her the perfect all-purpose flying British nanny in Robert Stevenson's **Mary Poppins** (1964). This was the

Far left: *'Wouldn't It Be Luverly' sings Audrey Hepburn as the cockney guttersnipe Eliza Doolittle in George Cukor's **My Fair Lady** (1964) in the huge Covent Garden set. Actually, Marni Nixon dubbed Audrey's singing for her.*

Left: *Rex Harrison, as the arrogant Professor Higgins in **My Fair Lady**, subjects Eliza to the tortures of elocution.*

Below: *Barbra Streisand (right), making her Oscar-winning screen debut in **Funny Girl** (1968), tries to stay upright during the 'Roller Skate Rag'. Barbra forced audiences to reassess their preconceived notions of beauty.*

only important original screen musical of the decade, although because of its animated sequence and high whimsical content, it is more to be considered alongside Disney's cartoon features. Since each one of these was an event, and despite the fact that **One Hundred and One Dalmatians** (1961) had been one of the best and most popular, Disney refused to consider roadshowing **Mary Poppins** — which nevertheless proved the biggest financial success of any Disney production.

Disney knew a good thing when he saw it, and was so impressed with the rushes of **Mary Poppins** that he invited other producers to view them. Before the film was released and won Andrews the Best Actress Oscar, she had signed for several more. One of these was **The Sound of Music** (1965), a mixture of nuns, Nazis and children, which had earned a reputation for being too saccharine during its 1959 Broadway run. The Rodgers and Hammerstein songs were the chief attraction for Hollywood and Rodgers struck a deal with 20th Century-Fox. William Wyler accepted the assignment and then changed his mind and it was given to Robert Wise on the strength of his **West Side Story** success. The screenplay was assigned to Ernest Lehman, who likewise had shown little affinity with screen sentiment. Even so, the cast and crew worked throughout in an attempt to rob the piece of its inherent stickiness, but it must be said that they weren't entirely successful. It may be because of its obvious faults that **The Sound of Music**'s virtues are all the more apparent, however. By far the greatest of these is Julie Andrews, who imbued her songs, lines and character with as much charm, merriment and wit as they would allow.

It was soon equally clear that the public loved **The Sound of Music** as they had loved no other film since **Gone With the Wind** a quarter of a century earlier. Just as **Doctor Zhivago**'s grosses wiped out MGM's memories of **Mutiny on the Bounty**, so was Fox able to forget **Cleopatra**. Even France liked **The Sound of Music**. As it knocked box-office records sideways, the industry breathed again. All it had to do — and it couldn't be too difficult, could it? — was to find a few more hits like **The Sound of Music**.

Above: *Julie Andrews (center, with hat), reached stardom as the singing governess to the Trapp children in the chocolate-box-office hit **The Sound of Music** (1965).*

Left: *Julie Andrews finally conquers the heart of Captain von Trapp (Christopher Plummer) and audiences almost everywhere in **The Sound of Music** helping the film to gross over $80 million.*

Below: *Ninety-nine helpless puppies, without their parents, cringe in terror as two evil kidnappers (or dognappers) search for them in **One Hundred And One Dalmatians** (1961).*

The Europeans

Chapter 2

The blockbuster habit was one of several reasons why attitudes to movies polarized in the Sixties: the art-houses were now booming and the trickle of films on television soon became a flood. The term "movie buff" was coined (replacing "fan"), and as likely as not the movies and the stars that buffs cared about came from Hollywood's past and Europe's present — in both cases without benefit of overtures, intervals and Technicolor.

The sweet life

In 1960, three impressive films arrived from Italy: Luchino Visconti's **Rocco and His Brothers**, Federico Fellini's **La Dolce Vita** and Michelangelo Antonioni's **L'Avventura**. All three directors had been making films since the Forties, but only Fellini was well known in America — although that does not explain why **La Dolce Vita** became the first foreign-language movie to appear among the top ten US box-office hits (if admittedly dubbed in many bookings) and, at $8 million rentals, remained unsurpassed until **I Am Curious – Yellow** (1967), not seen in the USA until 1969 for censorship reasons. It was an attraction for the increasing number of Americans who had spent their vacations in Europe — and had found it decadent. That had always been the message imparted by the Continental cinema, but the tourist industry gave it new impetus; **La Dolce Vita** confirmed the American view that Europeans were jaded, likely to consort with prostitutes and given to spending their evenings at joyless orgies.

The outlook of the other two films were equally bleak and just as pungently expressed. All three confirmed to critics and buffs the elementary fact that what the cinema needed was not wide screens but film-makers of vision and intelligence.

In France this view had emerged in the Fifties as the *auteur* theory, in which the most esteemed directors were those whose individual tastes and interests were discernible in their work. Alfred Hitchcock, for example, was accorded *auteur* status because he made thrillers with recurrent themes. Many of the most admired Hollywood film-makers of the time were quick to point out, however, that American movies were made, in collaboration, for worldwide mass consumption.

Elsewhere, however, there was a consistent individual tone to the work of certain directors, particularly those who wrote or contributed to their screenplays and sometimes did their own editing — among them Antonioni, Visconti, Fellini, Sweden's Ingmar Bergman, India's Satyajit Ray and the Spaniard Luis Buñuel.

*Taking an unconventional shower in the Trevi fountain is tall, voluptuous Swede Anita Ekberg, placed in a key position in Federico Fellini's frieze of decadent modern Rome, **La Dolce Vita** (1960).*

French inspiration

Those French critics who had evolved the theory in their writings were meanwhile putting it into practice by making movies on low budgets – a group that would be known as the *nouvelle vague,* or New Wave. Their films were chiefly made on location and with new or little-known talent – but the waves that resulted were very big. Francois Truffaut with **The 400 Blows** (1959), Jean-Luc Godard with **Breathless** (1960), Claude Chabrol with **Les Cousins** (1959), Alain Resnais with **Hiroshima Mon Amour** (1959) and Louis Malle with **The Lovers** (1958) tackled the job of movie-making with a vitality not to be found in Hollywood, and with only a fraction of Hollywood's resources – which suggested to some Americans that they might do the same.

The barrier to independent film-making in the USA had been the refusal of theaters to book any such movies; the Hollywood-owned circuits ignored "runaway" productions, while independent exhibitors were disinclined to offend Hollywood, their main suppliers. But the pattern of exhibition was now changing since there were sufficient art-house theaters for an independently produced movie to return its costs from them alone, provided those costs were low enough.

The producer Lewis M. Allen was the driving-force behind **The Connection** (1961) and **The Balcony** (1963), made for an average of $166,000, the latter with an investment from Walter Reade, a distributor of foreign movies, and with the participation of a Hollywood name, Shelley Winters, who received a share of the

Left: *Peter Falk (left), later 'Columbo', and Leonard Nimoy, later 'Mr. Spock', as very plain-clothed policemen in* **The Balcony** *(1963), based on Jean Genet's scurrilous play set in a brothel.*

Above: *Melina Mercouri, surrounded by friends and clients, used her mercurial temperament and ouzo-soaked voice to play one of the screen's first happy hookers in* **Never on Sunday** *(1960).*

Above: *Anthony Quinn (illustrated with Eleni Anousaki as a city prostitute) was the 'life force' hero **Zorba the Greek**, a role that seemed written for his ebullient personality.*

Left: *In **Zorba the Greek** (1964), set in Crete, a widow (Irene Papas) begins an affair with a visiting Englishman, and is murdered by the savage villagers, who blame her for the suicide of a lovesick and unsuccessful young suitor.*

profits. Both films were based on stage plays of minority appeal: **The Connection** was about drug-addicts waiting for their "fix"; **The Balcony** concerned the activities in a Continental brothel while a revolution waged outside. They did not point the way forward for independent American cinema, but two other films, Frank Perry's **David and Lisa** (1962) and Larry Peerce's **One Potato, Two Potato** (1964), did. The first was a tale of a young couple (Janet Margolin, Keir Dullea) falling in love in a mental home, and the second examined the difficulties affecting a mixed marriage.

In the age of blockbusters, these two low-key, starless, black-and-white dramas appealed to large numbers of moviegoers. Hollywood simply did not make movies like this any more — nor like **Never on Sunday** (1960), directed in Greece for $150,000 by an expatriate American, Jules Dassin, who also played one of the two leading roles, that of a prudish tourist who learns a thing or two about life from a happy hooker (Melina Mercouri, later Dassin's wife). The Cypriot director Michael Cacoyannis also made a Greek film — **Zorba the Greek** (1964) — in English, which was so popular that it appealed to audiences beyond the art-houses, partly due to the presence of Anthony Quinn in the title-role. Adapted from a novel by Nikos Kazantzakis, it featured Alan Bates as a prissy Anglo-Saxon who learns that there is a Mediterranean way of doing things — joyfully and extrovertedly — from an unconventional tutor, Zorba. Quinn's presence encouraged 20th Century-Fox to invest in the film; but Hollywood's interest in Europe was also due in part to an Italian actress who had become an international star.

After only a moderate success in Hollywood, Sophia Loren had returned to her native Italy at the start of the Sixties. Her husband, Carlo Ponti, had turned himself into one of the new Hollywood tycoons — and one whose main interest was in promoting Loren's international career. To that end he decided that she should make an Italian-speaking movie under the direction of Vittorio De Sica, the first Italian film-maker to achieve international fame.

Two Women (1961) was not on the level of such earlier De Sica masterpieces as **The Bicyle Thief** (1948) and **Umberto D** (1952), but it was a fine portrait of a woman managing to survive World War II. Loren received a Best Actress Oscar for her performance, perhaps because a dubbed version was widely seen in the US, but it was unprecedented for a non-American actress in a foreign-language film to receive that highest of prizes. Loren remained in Italy for two De Sica comedies co-starring Marcello Mastroianni, a "name" in the USA since he appeared in **La Dolce Vita**. In dubbed versions **Yesterday, Today and Tomorrow** (1964) and **Marriage — Italian Style** (1964) were happily received by American audiences, enabling Loren to return to Hollywood a much bigger star.

Below left: *Sylva Koscina manages to get her arms around muscleman Steve Reeves in* **Hercules Unchained** *(1960). The vogue for this type of film petered out in the mid-Sixties, to be replaced by the Spaghetti Western.*

Below: *After having been Mr America, Mr World and Mr Universe, it was natural that Steve Reeves (left) should flex his muscles in the title role of* **Hercules Unchained**, *one of a series of Italian-made torso-and-toga epics.*

The Italian way

Those three Loren movies were handled in the USA by a new, thrusting entrepreneur, Joseph E. Levine, who had made his reputation by buying the Stateside rights to a series of Italian epics starring an American muscle man, Steve Reeves, as the ancient Greek hero Hercules. **Hercules Unchained** (1960) was mediocre as spectacle or action-adventure, but Levine spent a million dollars to promote it — which paid dividends. Italian producers subsequently turned their attention to making more of these "sword-and-sandal" epics, and on the strength of their box-office success were able to lure such Hollywood names as Alan Ladd, Victor Mature, Guy Madison, Orson Welles, Lex Barker, Jeffrey Hunter, Debra Paget and Jeanne Crain to appear in them. But few of these stars were still greatly in demand out on the West Coast — and they were certainly not powerful enough to keep the series afloat when the paying public lost interest.

The Italian film industry had dreamed of beating Hollywood at its own game ever since the remarkable international success of the neorealist (and Communist) **The Bicycle Thief** in 1948, although it was a film that the Italian government and moguls both loathed; now

Top: *The Bible* (1966) contained some superb photography as in the scene from the 'Tower of Babel' episode illustrated.

Above: *Richard Harris as Cain suffers the wrath of God or that of director John Huston in* **The Bible** *, which tackled only the first 22 chapters of Genesis. Huston himself played Noah.*

Right: *Sophia Loren and Marlon Brando in a compromising situation on board an ocean liner in* **A Countess from Hong Kong** (1967), *the last film to be directed by Charles Chaplin. His ten-second appearance as a ship's steward was the best moment in the crude and unfunny comedy.*

Left: *Jane Fonda as the 40th-century astronaut **Barbarella** in the arms of angel John Phillip Law. Jane's then husband Roger Vadim managed to find various ways of getting his wife's clothes torn off during this 1968 comic-book extravaganza.*

Above: *Clint Eastwood made a name for himself as the taciturn 'Man with No Name' in Sergio Leone's first Spaghetti Western **A Fistful of Dollars** (1964), which took no less than $4.2 million in NA rentals.*

Left: *Louis Malle's second film **The Lovers** (1958) helped wreck sexual censorship the world over. The shots of an adulterous couple (Jeanne Moreau and Jean-Marc Bory) making love caused a sensation.*

they were conquering world markets with other movies which were very different. Some of the most popular came about as a result of Italian producers trying a few Westerns, shooting in Spain, where the scenery resembled the American West or Mexico. Second-rank stars such as Barker and Madison were easily persuaded to take lead roles. All these films were later named "Spaghetti Westerns".

The brighter producers realized that yesterday's movie stars were liable to be less attractive to audiences than current television heroes. Exported American Western series such as **Gunsmoke**, **Have Gun, Will Travel** and **Rawhide** were the rage throughout the Continent, and it was thought that Europeans would turn out to see their favorites in color and on the large screen.

From **Rawhide** came Clint Eastwood, who had not gone very far in Hollywood movies but after playing the deadly, monosyllabic gunfighter, the Man With No Name, for director Sergio Leone in three violent Westerns — **A Fistful of Dollars** (1964), **For a Few Dollars More** (1965) and **The Good, the Bad and the Ugly** (1966) — he was able to return to Hollywood as a major box-office star, eventually overtaking the likes of John Wayne and Steve McQueen.

Jane's comic strip

Another star to emerge at this time was Jane Fonda. Not yet having discovered politics or the extent of her talent, she was at first molded by the French director Roger Vadim (then her husband) into a sex object, in such films as the sci-fi spoof **Barbarella** (1968), based on a popular French comic strip. This was one of the typical "international"

Above: *French sex symbol Brigitte Bardot, known to the world simply as BB, pretty and kittenish as an unlikely revolutionary in Central America for Louis Malle's* **Viva Maria!** *(1965).*
Left: *Bardot and Jeanne Moreau (right) combined to sparkling effect in* **Viva Maria!** *As both girls were called Maria, the title referred to the two of them.*

movies of the decade, a co-production in English between Italy and France, with some money from Paramount, in return for US distribution rights.

The producer of **Barbarella** was Dino De Laurentiis, who was very active in this field. Having enjoyed a mild success with **Barabbas** (1962), a biblical epic directed by Richard Fleischer with Anthony Quinn heading the cast, De Laurentiis announced that he was tackling the Bible itself, in a film to be made by a consortium of directors, each handling a portion of his own choice — among them Orson Welles, Ingmar Bergman, Federico Fellini, Robert Bresson and John Huston.

In the event Huston tackled the whole project with a cast including George C. Scott, Ava Gardner, Peter O'Toole, Richard Harris and Huston himself as Noah — the guiding craftsmanship and imagination were of such a high order that **The Bible ... in the Beginning** (1966) was not unworthy to stand with Huston's finest work.

One episode depicted the Old Testament story of the Tower of Babel, whose image might be said to symbolize such coproductions at their worst. For instance, in De Sica's **The Condemned of Altona** (1963), one German family consisted of the American Fredric March and Robert Wagner, the Italian Sophia Loren, the Austrian-born Swiss Maximilian Schell and the French Françoise Prévost, all speaking with their own native accents. Based on a play by Jean-Paul Sartre, the film was an almost total disaster, as was the

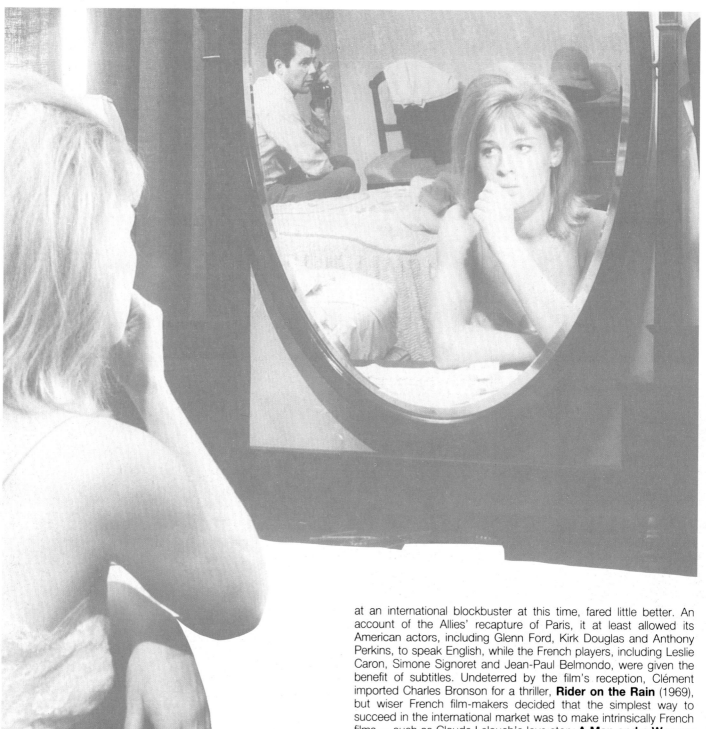

Above: *Julie Christie as the vain advertising model soars up the social ladder by using men such as TV interviewer Dirk Bogarde in John Schlesinger's cynical morality tale* **Darling** *(1965)...*
Right: *In* **The Spy Who Came in from the Cold** *(1965), British agent Leamas (Richard Burton), after a sentence in Wormwood Scrubs to embellish his track record as a drunken malcontent, is greeted by naive Communist librarian Liz (Claire Bloom), whom he also embroils in the plot — with fatal results.*

German director Bernhard Wicki's 1964 adaptation of Friedrich Dürrenmatt's **The Visit**, starring Ingrid Bergman and Anthony Quinn.

René Clément's **Is Paris Burning?** (1966), France's one attempt at an international blockbuster at this time, fared little better. An account of the Allies' recapture of Paris, it at least allowed its American actors, including Glenn Ford, Kirk Douglas and Anthony Perkins, to speak English, while the French players, including Leslie Caron, Simone Signoret and Jean-Paul Belmondo, were given the benefit of subtitles. Undeterred by the film's reception, Clément imported Charles Bronson for a thriller, **Rider on the Rain** (1969), but wiser French film-makers decided that the simplest way to succeed in the international market was to make intrinsically French films — such as Claude Lelouch's love story **A Man and a Woman** (1966), which became (until **La Cage aux Folles**, 1979) the highest-grossing French-language movie ever to play in American theaters.

Viva Maria! (1965) attracted immediate international attention because it teamed France's contrasting sex-symbols, Brigitte Bardot and the intellectual's favorite, Jeanne Moreau. United Artists supplied some of the budget and the leading man, George Hamilton, but Louis Malle's film with the two ladies scampering about Mexico during one or other of its revolutions, was a damp squib. Another New Wave director, François Truffaut, turned up in Britain because no French producer would finance his version of Ray Bradbury's **Fahrenheit 451** (1966), but despite the presence of Julie Christie in two roles, Universal did not get a hefty return on its investment.

The British bubble

Britain, in fact, was where the action was. American producers,

directors, writers and actors poured into the UK to help in the revival of the British film industry, which was being spearheaded by Woodfall, the company founded by director Tony Richardson and playwright John Osborne. The public endorsed two Woodfall productions, **Saturday Night and Sunday Morning** (1960) and **A Taste of Honey** (1961), the first of which brought the forceful young proletarian actor Albert Finney to the fore. Woodfall decided Finney was ideal for the title-role of **Tom Jones** (1963), based on Henry Fielding's bawdy eighteenth-century novel. This ambitious historical subject required a bigger budget than Woodfall was used to, but when none was forthcoming from British sources United Artists stepped in. **Tom Jones** opened in the USA to critical acclaim, played to capacity houses and went on to win Oscars for Best Film, Best Director (Richardson) and Best Screenplay (Osborne).

Those Oscars were the final shots in the Woodfall revolution. British cinema would never be the same again, although Hollywood was keen enough to back movies about the British working class, many of which were very bad. Two which were extremely good — made

Right: *Albert Finney (right) as* **Tom Jones** *with Diane Cilento (then the wife of Sean Connery) in one of the many amorous adventures rollickingly portrayed in Tony Richardson's 1963 Oscar-winning British triumph.*

Below: *Finney in one of the few quiet and chaste moments with Susannah York as Sophia Western, the girl he marries after his wild oats are sown.*

without American backing — were directed by John Schlesinger, **A Kind of Loving** (1962) and **Billy Liar** (1963), which respectively starred Alan Bates and Tom Courtenay.

The latter film also contained the first major appearance of a pretty, friendly blonde girl, Julie Christie, who proved to be ideal for Schlesinger's next film, **Darling . . .** (1965), the story of a London model scripted by Frederic Raphael. Dirk Bogarde was hired as her costar but not until a part was written in for Laurence Harvey — an English actor who had attracted some attention in America — was backing secured, partly because this exposé of the morals of London's fashion world was not quite what was expected of British movies at this time. In the event, Christie's performance as the promiscuous heroine won her the Best Actress Oscar, and Schlesinger had no difficulty finding backing for his next venture, **Far From the Madding Crowd** (1967), a version of Thomas Hardy's novel. Bates, Christie, Peter Finch and Terence Stamp were cast and MGM put up the money, but the film was not a great success in the USA.

Lynn and Vanessa Redgrave competed for Oscars for their roles in two of the better post-Woodfall films. Karel Reisz's **Morgan: a Suitable Case for Treatment** (1966), starring Vanessa as a society wife, has dated badly, however. American audiences were just not interested in the character of her husband, crazy Morgan (David Warner). But they loved **Georgy Girl** (1966) – featuring Lynn as an ugly duckling who blossoms when she realizes that she's found attractive by both her elderly guardian (James Mason) and the cast-off lover (Alan Bates) of her bitchy flat-mate (Charlotte Rampling). The film's frank treatment of sex was one reason why it became a top-ten box-office hit in the US. Backed by Paramount, **Alfie** (1966), in which a cockney layabout (Michael Caine) uses a number of women before tossing them aside like Kleenex, echoed its box-office success.

Although Shelley Winters was brought over to Britain for **Alfie**, it wasn't intended for the international market in quite the same way as the two movies that made Michael Caine a star, **Zulu** (1963), a spectacular re-creation of the battle of Rorke's Drift filmed in South Africa with Stanley Baker and Jack Hawkins, and **The Ipcress File** (1965). The latter, a spy thriller, was set in London, but it was the kind of glossy entertainment that had previously been the domain of Hollywood. It typified a trend in the Sixties for location-shooting in Europe, the Americans taking full advantage of the skills available in the British industry in particular.

Also, the American film industry liked the new generation of British stars. Hollywood had always poached talent from wherever it could be found, and had assimilated many British stars and character

Right: *Sean Connery as British agent James Bond in* **Dr. No** *(1962) in the first of a string of car chases that were to become a staple ingredient of the seemingly endless series.*

Below: *32-year-old Sean Connery gained international stardom in* **Dr. No**, *the first of over a dozen James Bond pictures, the most durable of all long-running, money-spinning movie series. Twenty-one years later, Connery was again playing 007.*

actors through the years. What is more puzzling is why Hollywood liked British directors, few of whom carried much prestige. Clearly, Hollywood had first call on big names like Carol Reed, David Lean and later John Schlesinger, but many other Brits had long careers working for the Americans without managing more than a couple of box-office hits apiece. Columbia employed J. Lee Thompson to direct **The Guns of Navarone** (1961) and 20th Century-Fox gave **Those Magnificent Men in Their Flying Machines** (1965) to Ken Annakin, perhaps on the precedent of Michael Anderson directing **Around the World in 80 Days** (1956). Both movies owed their popularity to their powerful casts: Gregory Peck, David Niven, Anthony Quayle, Anthony Quinn and Stanley Baker in **Navarone**, a tale of saboteurs working in Greece during the German occupation; and Sarah Miles, Stuart Whitman, James Fox, Robert Morley among many more in **Those Magnificent Men**, a lavish — but unamusing — comedy about the 1910 London to Paris air race. Few critics would go to bat for Terence Young, who directed the first James Bond film, **Doctor No** (1962), which, unlike the two films just mentioned was not expected to do more than moderately well.

The greatest Bond

The 007 series, however, became the most successful in the history of the cinema. Bond, an urbane, well-dressed secret service man often pitted against other agents in exotic locales, and with a taste for fast cars and fast women, had been introduced by novelist Ian Fleming in 1952, but was not an immediate success. Each of the Bond books, though, did better than the one before, and they were enjoying respectable sales by the end of the decade. The decision to make a Bond movie was taken by producers Harry Saltzman, a Canadian who had provided Woodfall's finance, and Albert ("Cubby") Broccoli, an American who had been making mediocre action films in Britain for a few years. Young, best known for violent melodramas, was hired to direct.

Among the actors who turned down the role of Bond were Trevor Howard, Peter Finch and David Niven. It went to Sean Connery, who lacked the necessary suavity and polish but acquired these qualities as time went by. **Dr No**, a surprise hit, made major stars of him and Ursula Andress, and necessitated another 007 vehicle, **From Russia With Love** (1964) — and with that America joined Britain in Bond fever. **Goldfinger** (1964), **Thunderball** (1965) and **You Only Live Twice** (1967) were all box-office bonanzas, although Connery griped against the producers' greed and refused to do **On Her Majesty's Secret Service** (1969). He was replaced by George Lazenby, an Australian who was unknown then and has been ever since. Saltzman and Broccoli were soon petitioning Connery to return.

Saltzman had also produced **The Ipcress File**, whose secret service hero Harry Palmer was, as played by Michael Caine and more

Below: **Help!** *(1965) was an Eastmancolor package for the Beatles, full of visual tricks displayed by director Richard Lester, and crammed with some of their best numbers.*

Below: *'All You Need Is Love', one of the many Beatles' hits animated in* **Yellow Submarine** *(1968).*

Left: *Peter Sellers demonstrated his versatility in a triple role in* **Dr. Strangelove or How I Learned to Stop Worrying and Love the Bomb** *(1963) as an RAF officer, the US President and the mad nuclear scientist (illustrated) of the title.*

Below: **The Guns of Navarone** *(1961). Playing a team of saboteurs were (from left to right) Anthony Quinn, Gia Scala (as a traitor), Stanley Baker, Gregory Peck, David Niven and James Darren.*

realistically written by Len Deighton, the antithesis of Bond; two sequels, **Funeral in Berlin** (1966) and **Billion Dollar Brain** (1967), did respectably, but while Bond carried on Harry Palmer was quietly put out to grass.

In the pink

A further series began with **The Pink Panther** (1963), directed by Blake Edwards and starring Peter Sellers as Inspector Clouseau. This bumbling French police detective took the public fancy sufficiently for Edwards to incorporate the character in **A Shot in the Dark** (1964), which was an even bigger success. Neither Edwards nor Sellers had anything to do with **Inspector Clouseau** (1969), in which the role was played by Alan Arkin for director Bud Yorkin, but they gave the character a whirl in the Seventies when their careers weren't going too well, with profitable results.

Along with **Lawrence of Arabia** and Julie Andrews, Sellers — a comic with a gift for mimicry — was a factor in Hollywood's interest in Britain in the Sixties, but the biggest attractions were Woodfall, **Tom Jones**, James Bond and the Beatles. Although the Liverpool pop group appeared in only two fictional features, **A Hard Day's Night** (1964) and **Help!** (1965), both directed by the American Richard Lester, the first of these was a worldwide hit, which emphasized the growing appeal of movies for the young (as older audiences fell away) at this time.

Below left: *The age of Vladimir Nabokov's nymphet **Lolita** (1962) was raised, thus giving 16-year-old Sue Lyon the chance to make her screen debut opposite James Mason and Peter Sellers.*

Below right: *'How could they make a movie of **Lolita**?' asked the posters. Stanley Kubrick managed very well, and the takings were boosted by pictures like this one of Sue Lyon in the title role.*

Below: *James Mason as Nabokov's Humbert Humbert helps to satisfy his 'perverse passion' for young girls by painting the toenails of Sue Lyon as **Lolita**.*

Above: *The only British-born-and-bred musical to win the Best Picture Oscar was* **Oliver!** *(1968), Carol Reed's well-scrubbed version of the musical based on Dickens, starring Oliver Reed (foreground left, the director's nephew) as Bill Sikes, Shani Wallis (center) as Nancy and nine-year-old Mark Lester in the title role.*

Far left: *British stage actor Paul Scofield, in only his fourth film in 12 years, as Sir Thomas More, Chancellor of England, in* **A Man for All Seasons** *(1966). Orson Welles played Cardinal Wolsey.*

Left: *Paul Scofield (right) as Sir Thomas More, a man of conscience, confronts Robert Shaw's King Henry VIII in Fred Zinnemann's well-acted historical drama.*

Another American active in Britain was Stanley Donen, whose **Two for the Road** (1967) engagingly shunted Albert Finney and Audrey Hepburn around France as a couple falling in and out of love and marriage. Stanley Kubrick's film of Nabokov's novel **Lolita** (1962), starring James Mason as the middle-aged hero with a penchant for under-age girls, was made in Britain because its risqué subject matter might mean low box-office returns and costs therefore had to be kept down. Kubrick wasn't entirely successful in making the Home Counties look like the Midwest, but he stayed on for one of the decade's critical triumphs, **Dr Strangelove, or How I Learned to Stop Worrying and Love the Bomb** (1964), an anti-nuclear black comedy mostly set in America and featuring George C. Scott with Peter Sellers in three roles. When Fred Zinnemann left Hollywood to settle in Britain, he directed **A Man for All Seasons** (1966), based on Robert Bolt's historical play about the clash between Sir Thomas More (Paul Scofield) and Henry VIII (Robert Shaw). It won the Best Film Oscar, Zinnemann was voted Best Director and Scofield was Best Actor.

In 1968, Carol Reed's musical **Oliver!**, made in Britain, won the Best Film Oscar and Reed the Best Director. He was followed a year later by fellow-Londoner John Schlesinger, but for a film made in New York — **Midnight Cowboy**, also chosen as Best Film of its year.

American stars who worked in England in the Sixties included Judy Garland, making her final bow playing an American singer appearing at the London Palladium in Ronald Neame's **I Could Go On Singing** (1963); and Bahamian Sidney Poitier, who became a British West Indian teacher at an East End school in **To Sir, With Love** (1967). Charles Chaplin directed Marlon Brando — an unhappy collaboration — and Sophia Loren in **A Countess From Hong Kong** (1967), although the result was in inverse proportion to the publicity engendered. The Polish director Roman Polanski set the French actress Catherine Deneuve in South Kensington for the decade's most disturbing horror story, **Repulsion** (1965).

Franco Zeffirelli's **Romeo and Juliet** (1968) was shot in his native Italy but it was otherwise a British film with a British cast. Michelangelo Antonioni came to London, however, for **Blow-Up** (1967), another youth movie that found a warm reception wherever it was shown. Starring David Hemmings as a successful photographer discovering the emptiness of his "Swinging London" existence, **Blow-Up** — in its mixture of chic, disillusion, mystery and sexual experimentation — may be the quintessential movie of the Sixties; surprisingly, it is also one of the least dated.

Left: *The legendary Judy Garland making her final screen appearance in the hackneyed British musical* **I Could Go On Singing** *(1963), almost a parody of her own private and public life.*

Right: *A scene from Franco Zeffirelli's bustling, energetic, and colorful 1968 version of Shakespeare's* **Romeo and Juliet**.

Below: *Jane Birkin (right) and Gillian Hills (left) romp in the nude with 'Swinging London' photographer David Hemmings in Michelangelo Antonioni's trendy puzzler* **Blow-Up** *(1967).*

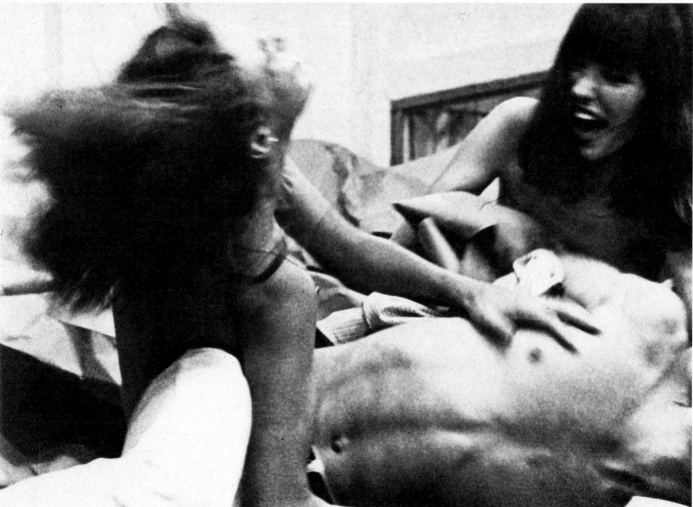

Pillow Talk

Chapter 3

Sex, from **La Dolce Vita** to **Blow-Up**, and not forgetting Brigitte Bardot, **The Lovers**, **Georgy Girl** and **Alfie**, was a European phenomenon – despite the inroads made by Hollywood into the greater American consciousness in the Fifties. Films were made of Broadway plays and bestselling novels, with their producers fighting every step of the way to preserve the sexual frankness that in many cases had been the reason for their popularity. The Motion Picture Association of America (MPAA), guardian of the movies' morals since the effective implementation of the Hays Code in 1934, was beginning to give ground, to the extent that, for the first time since then, it was clear that when a man chased a woman on the screen he was more interested in bedding than wedding her.

Bachelor boys

In comedy, it was the time of the swinging bachelor, invariably equipped with a luxurious pad replete with a vast bed and a stock of champagne in the icebox. Lovers and would-be lovers included Frank Sinatra, Dean Martin, Jack Lemmon, Tony Curtis and most notably Rock Hudson, whose pictures with Doris Day – **Pillow Talk** (1959), **Lover Come Back** (1961), **Send Me No Flowers** (1964) – were among the biggest hits of the era. She also costarred with Cary Grant (**That Touch of Mink**, 1962), James Garner (**The Thrill of It All** and **Move Over Darling**, both 1963) and Rod Taylor (**The Glass Bottom Boat**, 1966) and eventually became the butt of many a nightclub comic's joke for retaining her virginity through so many pictures. There was rough justice in this, despite her natural personality and comic skill, for the tone of these films is at best bland and at worse salacious – an anesthetized *Playboy* view of sex. Jane Fonda, Shirley MacLaine and Natalie Wood were among the girls tempted to toss away their virginity in movies: Peter Tewkesbury's **Sunday in New York** (1964), starring Fonda, is virtually the sole film of this time and type which doesn't leer or smirk.

Two serious films with a comic point of view were Blake Edwards' **Breakfast at Tiffany's** (1961), in which Audrey Hepburn is a kookie New Yorker available at the right price, and Arthur Hiller's **The Americanization of Emily** (1964), with Julie Andrews as a British girl wondering how best to please an American soldier (James Garner) in wartime. The best sex comedy of the period was Billy Wilder's **The Apartment** (1960), full of inspired comic lines and sadness. Both Jack Lemmon, as a junior executive hoping for advancement by loaning his superiors the key to his rooms, and

Right: *Rock Hudson and Doris Day in* **Send Me No Flowers** *(1964), the last of three fluffy comedies they made together. In the light of Hudson's death in 1985, the plot about a husband who believes he's dying, and determines to find his wife another mate, has lost some of its humor.*

Shirley MacLaine, as one of the girls being taken there, surpassed themselves in this highly popular film, winner of the Best Film, Best Director and Best Original Screenplay Oscars.

For many years, Wilder and fellow Hollywood directors like William Wyler and George Stevens had been fighting against the restrictions of the MPAA — but none more so than Wilder, who used the triumph of **The Apartment** and 1959's **Some Like It Hot** to smooth the way for the filming of **Irma La Douce** (1963), a comedy about a Parisian hooker (MacLaine) and her policeman lover (Lemmon), whose baby she bears on the church steps just after they've married. The subject was sanctioned inasmuch as the original show had been a great success in Paris, London and New York. The public loved the film — ironically, for it is one of Wilder's poorest movies, while his next two, among his most brilliant work, were rejected.

Critics thought he had gone too far with **Kiss Me Stupid** (1964) and panned it; it shares with **The Fortune Cookie** (1966) a cynical view of American society which Lyndon B. Johnson's America found unpalatable. In the first, a small town amateur songwriter (Ray Walston) so wants to make it big that he is prepared to offer a hooker (Kim Novak), masquerading as his wife, to a visiting TV celebrity (Dean Martin) — only his real wife changes place with her. The second film is less overtly sexual, but concludes with a white man (Lemmon) and a black football player going off into the sunset together; they aren't necessarily in love, but the black guy has shown no interest in women, while Lemmon's wife is portrayed as viciously greedy.

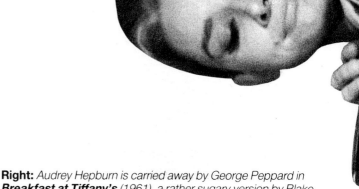

Below: *Nebbish executive Jack Lemmon (left) drowns his sorrows in Billy Wilder's brilliant acid comedy* **The Apartment** *(1960) while waiting to get home. He lends his apartment to his superiors to entertain their lady friends. The film was the last black-and-white movie to win the Best Picture Oscar.*

Right: *Audrey Hepburn is carried away by George Peppard in* **Breakfast at Tiffany's** *(1961), a rather sugary version by Blake Edwards of the Truman Capote novella.*

Gays were beginning to be portrayed in movies, if only tentatively. Homosexuality in someone's past was the key to blackmail in two political dramas, **Advise and Consent** and **The Best Man** (1964), while lesbianism was an accusation thrown about in Wyler's **The Children's Hour** (1962), with Audrey Hepburn and Shirley Mac-Laine. (When Wyler had originally filmed Lillian Hellman's play, as **These Three** in 1936, a heterosexual premarital affair substituted for lesbianism.) The film's failure to find a public seemed to suggest that the public didn't wish to see "deviant" behavior on the screen — and it wasn't until **The Group** (1966) that an affair between two women was explicitly acknowledged. The film's director was Sidney Lumet, who also persuaded the MPAA to allow him to show a woman baring her breasts in **The Pawnbroker** (1965) — the first time such a sight had been seen in an American film since the ethnic **Tabu** in 1931. The cause on this occasion was serious, for the picture was a harsh and powerful study of the survivor of a Nazi concentration camp.

Above and right: *Rod Steiger in his favorite role as* ***The Pawnbroker*** *(1965) an ex-concentration camp victim now living in Spanish Harlem and tortured by his memories. It was shot on location in New York by Sidney Lumet.*

Left: *Anne Jackson and Walter Matthau in* ***The Secret Life of an American Wife*** *(1968), a sharp satire on surburban American mores. Jackson, primarily a stage actress, appears as a bored housewife seeking extramarital kicks with a movie star.*

Above: *The highest paid and most publicized couple in the movies, Elizabeth Taylor and Richard Burton, as the foul-mouthed and self-loathing George and Martha in the best of the ten films they made together,* **Who's Afraid Of Virginia Woolf?** *(1966).*

Far left: *The tragic and lovely Marilyn Monroe on the set of her last completed film,* **The Misfits** *(1961). A week before the opening, she divorced Arthur Miller, who wrote the script.*

Left: *Susannah York as one of the exhausted contestants of the Hollywood dance marathons held during the Depression evoked by Sydney Pollack in* **They Shoot Horses Don't They?** *(1969).*

In the meantime, Natalie Wood had starred in two films which dealt with premarital sex, as it affected high school kids in the Twenties in Elia Kazan's **Splendor in the Grass** (1961), and as a Macy's clerk who reluctantly plans an abortion until prevented at the last minute by her repentant lover (Steve McQueen) in Robert Mulligan's **Love With the Proper Stranger** (1963). Nor could there be any doubt that Clark Gable and Marilyn Monroe were playing lovers in the full sense of the word in John Huston's **The Misfits** (1961). Her last completed film, it was written by her then husband Arthur Miller, whose Broadway contemporaries, notably Tennessee Williams, had contributed to Hollywood's losing its prudishness during the Fifties. Williams' **Sweet Bird of Youth** (1962), directed by Richard Brooks, was not the equal of his earlier films like **A Streetcar Named Desire** (1951) and **Suddenly Last Summer** (1959), but its aging actress heroine (Geraldine Page) *is* allowed her gigolo (Paul Newman). Similarly, **Breakfast at Tiffany's** had a hero (George Peppard) being kept by an older woman (Patricia Neal).

Breaking taboos

Irving Wallace, who wrote the novel on which **The Chapman Report** (1962) was based, was no Tennessee Williams or Arthur Miller, but the film's director, George Cukor, was one of the Hollywood elite, and its producer, Darryl F. Zanuck, was determined to repeat the success of an earlier filmed bestseller, **Peyton Place** (1957), by retaining its raciness. The report in question concerned sexual behavior, and the film was able to deal with the rare topics of frigidity, nymphomania, adultery and gang-rape.

Another important Broadway dramatist, Edward Albee, provided four-letter-word-littered dialogue in **Who's Afraid of Virginia Woolf?** (1966), as a professor (Richard Burton) and his wife (Elizabeth Taylor) hurl abuse at each other throughout one long drunken night. Mike Nichols directed this watershed film, and he went on to make **The Graduate** (1967), in which a young man (Dustin Hoffman), returning from college, is seduced by a friend (Anne Bancroft) of his parents. **The Graduate** was not raunchy; but its frankness and dialogue would not have been permitted even a few years earlier.

*Below: After eight years of struggle to make a living out of acting, 30-year-old Dustin Hoffman (right) became a star overnight as 20-year-old Benjamin Braddock, **The Graduate** in Mike Nichols' 1967 film. Ben falls in love with the daughter (Katharine Ross) of the woman who seduced him, and pursues her to Berkeley with offers of marriage. **Left:** Middle-class college kids went for the story in a big way, the boys identifying with rebel Hoffman, who rescues Ross from a respectable marriage in the nick of time.*

As audiences everywhere reveled in this new freedom, it was clear that the MPAA restrictions had to be removed. The huge popularity of **Bonnie and Clyde** (1967) was another contributory factor to this, for Arthur Penn's clever gangster thriller, starring Warren Beatty and Faye Dunaway, contained more blood and violence than had been seen before in a major movie.

The point is that audiences were leaving their TV sets to see these films, as well as British equivalents like **Georgy Girl** and **Alfie**. They also gave a warm welcome to **Rachel, Rachel** (1968), directed by Paul Newman and starring his wife Joanne Woodward as a small-town teacher who has a last sexual fling before settling into spinsterhood; lesbianism was hinted at in this film, too.

The public meanwhile gave a more guarded reception to **The Killing of Sister George** (1968); based on a British play which had enjoyed a long run on Broadway, it was the story of a bossy radio soap-opera queen (Beryl Reid) who loses her girlfriend (Susannah York) to a predatory BBC executive (Coral Browne).

Left: ***The Killing of Sister George*** *(1968) dealt with a lesbian relationship between Beryl Reid (left) as a bad-tempered soap-opera actress and Susannah York (right) as her child-like lover.*

Right: *Paul Newman's first film as director,* ***Rachel, Rachel*** *(1968) was the perfect vehicle for his wife Joanne Woodward, as a repressed Connecticut schoolteacher.*

Below: *Faye Dunaway and Warren Beatty as bank robbers* ***Bonnie and Clyde*** *(1967). Caught in an ambush, they barely escape with their lives — but they will be less lucky next time.*

Two discreet films on male homosexuality failed to attract viewers, however. John Huston's **Reflections in a Golden Eye** (1967), based on the novel by Carson McCullers and set in the Deep South, and John Flynn's **The Sergeant** (1968), set in northern France and very different in tone, share the theme of an officer conceiving an almighty passion for an enlisted man. Marlon Brando played the man obsessed in Huston's film, where matters are complicated by the fact that he has a wife (Elizabeth Taylor).

By this time, the MPAA had scrapped its regulations. Much had happened to American film-making since that flurry of independent production in the early Sixties. The independents were supplying movies in English to both art-houses and the seedy exploitation theaters which had become starved of product since TV had forced the closure of Hollywood's Poverty Row studios; Westerns and other action films had been replaced by what often amounted to soft

Left: 23-year-old Jane Fonda, making her screen debut in **Tall Story** (1960), is shocked to find an unclothed Tom Laughlin, team mate of her basketball star husband Anthony Perkins (right), in their apartment. It was a far cry from Ms Fonda's later roles.

Bottom left: A dramatic moment from John Huston's **Reflections In A Golden Eye** (1967) as Elizabeth Taylor lashes at her husband Marlon Brando, who has been out trying to ride his wife's stallion to prove his virility. Brando's lack of horsemanship is linked to the character's closet homosexuality.

Right: Curvacious American sex-symbol of the 60s Raquel Welch used her anatomy to effect in the grunt 'n' groan prehistoric saga **One Million Years B.C.** (1966), wearing a Stone-Age designer bikini.

pornography. In the Fifties, only a handful of maverick exhibitors were prepared to show movies denied the MPAA seal of approval, but such films had multiplied and were bringing customers back to the theaters.

The MPAA bravely announced that it was renouncing the Code because patrons were now sufficiently sophisticated to decide what they and their children could be permitted to see, but the truth was that sex had always sold tickets and was doing so more than ever when the cinema was in desperate need of support. Chancing their arms, the owners of exploitation houses offered hardcore pornography, and when they weren't prosecuted this became a staple diet — if for a while creating havoc in newspaper offices as discussions raged as to whether such films should be reviewed or advertised.

For Hollywood this was a bewildering time, but it eventually came up with three eminently respectable films with a strong sexual content. Larry Peerce's **Goodbye, Columbus** (1969), based on Philip Roth's novel, starred Richard Benjamin and Ali MacGraw as a young, unmarried Jewish couple who enjoy their lovemaking (and discuss contraception); Paul Mazursky's **Bob & Carol & Ted & Alice** (1969) had two couples abortively engaged in wife-swapping after

Left: *Clive Donner's now dated hit* **What's New, Pussycat?** *(1965) is notable as Woody Allen's debut as writer and performer. Peter O'Toole, as an English playboy and editor of a fashion magazine, is engaged to be married but is constantly distracted by leggy ladies such as aviatrix Ursula Andress.* **Above:** *Professional stripper Paula Prentiss and enthusiastic amateur O'Toole entertain at Paris's Crazy Horse Saloon in* **What's New, Pussycat?**

Top left: *Bette Davis (right) as a drunken ex-child star gets her kicks by slowly torturing her crippled sister Joan Crawford (left) in Robert Aldrich's* **What Ever Happened to Baby Jane?** *(1962). It was the only time the two former Warner Bros. stars appeared together.*

trying a little adultery on the side; and John Schlesinger's **Midnight Cowboy** (1969) starred Dustin Hoffman as a tubercular hustler and Jon Voight as a country boy who comes to New York to set himself up as a gigolo for Park Avenue ladies, but finds his only paying customers are gays.

All three films were enormously popular, as was Dennis Hopper's **Easy Rider** (1969), which followed two drugged-up hippies (Hopper and Peter Fonda) as they travel across the country, ostensibly to deliver drugs but in fact on a voyage of discovery. They have a psychedelic trip while making love to two girls (Karen Black and Toni

Left: *Tennessee Williams' plays were often adapted to the screen in the 60s, and John Huston's* **The Night Of The Iguana** *(1964) was an engrossing example. Among the cast were Richard Burton (left) and Sue Lyon (right).*

Right: *Richard Benjamin and Ali MacGraw take a shower in* **Goodbye, Columbus** *(1969), based on Philip Roth's stinging portrait of Jewish life in the Bronx in the 1950s.*

Below: **Bob & Carol & Ted & Alice** *(1969) was a comedy about surburban wife-swapping in which the two couples realize that love and fidelity are more important than sex. Here Elliott Gould and an air hostess plan adultery in the air.*

Above: *Paul Newman (right) as the cynical, irresponsible* **Hud** *(1963), billed as 'the man with the barbed wire soul!' Here he gets his teenage brother Brandon de Wilde drunk before returning to their declining cattle ranch.*

Left: *Jon Voight, a young hustler from Texas, the* **Midnight Cowboy** *(1969) of the title, thinks he has it made when he services the wealthy lady, Sylvia Miles, he meets on 5th Avenue.* **Top near left:** *Dustin Hoffman took on the character role of Ratso, the petty conman. With his greasy hair, pallid complexion, bad teeth and gammy leg, he merged perfectly into the seamy New York setting of the movie.*

Top far left: *In her decaying Hollywood mansion, Bette Davis as the demented ex-child star Jane Hudson tries to answer the question of the title,* **What Ever Happened to Baby Jane?** *(1962), by rehearsing her comeback act with the portly Victor Buono, making his film debut, at the piano.*

Basil) in a cemetery, encounter a mild-mannered lawyer (Jack Nicholson) who finds their lifestyle irresistible, and discover that the *real* America belongs to rednecks only too eager to cut down anyone not conforming to *their* way of life.

Hopper, who directed with feeling, and Fonda were known to have adopted a hippie existence offscreen. Public curiosity about that lifestyle, together with the innate romanticism of the film, may have been why it was so popular.

It was easy to understand why a whole generation of young Americans had revolted against their parents' values. Despite the Vietnam War and the assassinations of John Kennedy, Bobby Kennedy and Martin Luther King, institutional America was well content with itself. Yet the young did not care for its materialism, for the bland, dishonest pap always available on the home screen, and above all for US involvement in Vietnam. In New York, the rallying cry came from a rock musical, *Hair*; **Easy Rider** too spoke to hippies everywhere.

Hair owed much of its notoriety to the fact that it climaxed with naked girls and boys dancing on the stage. The sex scenes in **Easy Rider** were not so explicit, nor even erotic, involving casual couplings with glamorized hookers rather than the grand romances of Bogart and Bergman, Garbo and Taylor, or Gable and Crawford, the staple diet of the Thirties and Forties. Hollywood was very uncertain about its new license to show overt sexual acts.

As the industry studied the film's relatively huge receipts (ultimate domestic rentals alone of over $19 million on a derisory outlay of $400,000, a percentage profit virtually unheard of in Hollywood history), the future seemed clear … and simple. **Easy Rider** was no great work of art; neither was Hopper a Wyler or a Cukor. Surely it would not be difficult to make better films to pull in even bigger profits. But, in fact, apart from its pleasing if comparatively anodyne stepchild **American Graffiti** (1973) — which actually took almost three times as much at the box-office — **Easy Rider** remained a tantalizing one-off. The other imitations were abysmal flops and artistic disasters.

The Secret of Success

Chapter 4

While Hollywood wondered how best to keep its audiences, Walt Disney's studio had no such problems. Disney turned out a series of live-action family comedies which one after the other rang box-office bells – from **The Absent-Minded Professor** (1961) to **The Love Bug** (1969), the adventures of an independent-minded Volkswagen. By the end of the decade, however, a Disney movie was no longer guaranteed to be a hit. Family audiences had disappeared.

Shock waves

The greatest shock waves followed in the wake of **The Sound of Music**. Two family movies, **Dr Dolittle** (1967) and **Chitty Chitty Bang Bang** (1968), promptly failed. Julie Andrews had a big success with a frothy musical set in the Twenties, **Thoroughly Modern Millie** (1967), but audiences quickly fell away for both **Star!** (1968), in which she played the temperamental stage actress Gertrude Lawrence, and **Darling Lili** (1969), a World War I spy spoof, costarring Rock Hudson. In both instances the quality of the material was in doubt, and **Darling Lili** in particular was a long, lumbering yawn as directed by Blake Edwards.

As the leading lady of musicals, Andrews had a new challenger in Barbra Streisand, who scored a big hit when she re-created her Broadway role of comedienne Fanny Brice in **Funny Girl** (1968), directed by William Wyler. But her next film, **Hello Dolly!**, another adaptation from Broadway, failed to recoup its very high budget.

British singer Petula Clark, whose records were hot sellers throughout Europe, played opposite Peter O'Toole in a musical version of **Goodbye Mr Chips** (1969), and starred with Fred Astaire and Tommy Steele in **Finian's Rainbow** (1968); the first did badly after undeservedly poor notices, but the second did only average business after very good ones.

Clark's popularity in Europe was expected to compensate for the Continent's indifference to musicals, and on that principle Jean Seberg was cast in **Paint Your Wagon** (1969), which, like **My Fair Lady**, was based on an old Lerner-Loewe Broadway show. Seberg was an American actress who had found fame in such French movies as **Breathless**, and was therefore expected to guarantee the success of the film in Europe. Starring with her were two box-office giants, Clint Eastwood and Lee Marvin, but **Paint Your Wagon** still took less than $15 million in US rentals – though in Britain Marvin had a Number 1 hit single with "Wandering Star" (ironically, since it was put together syllable by syllable from Marvin's

Right: Audiences were pleased to say **Goodbye Mr Chips** (1969), after 147 minutes of this big budget musical weepie. Peter O'Toole and Petula Clark (among the boatered boys) could in no way replace Robert Donat and Greer Garson of the 1939 version.

innumerable attempts at singing it for the soundtrack). This was, indeed, an era when musicals were likely to include stars who could neither sing nor dance — Vanessa Redgrave, for example, in another film of a Lerner-Loewe Broadway musical, **Camelot** (1967), which did only moderately well ($14 million). But the biggest flop of all, **Sweet Charity** (1969), starred a popular and very talented singer-dancer, Shirley MacLaine, and ironically received sparkling notices! The public was right, however — the last half-hour of **Sweet Charity** is a real downer, likely to send even the greatest optimist out into the street depressed.

The failure or half-failure of this batch of musicals may be attributable to a dozen different reasons, from the dreary scores of **Dr Dolittle** and **Goodbye Mr Chips** to the fact that the public didn't care to see Julie Andrews playing a vamp. Perhaps the main reason was that they generally lacked the élan and high spirits of Hollywood's musicals of the Thirties and Forties. Also, the musical was a form that had become dangerously expensive — so that if a musical couldn't succeed in roadshow engagements, it couldn't succeed at all. During the Seventies, Hollywood ventured to make only a handful of musicals, none of which revived the genre.

Perhaps the last successful non-musical roadshow was **Hawaii** (1966), again with Julie Andrews; but no one considered showing the sequel, **The Hawaiians** (1970), in this way. **The Sand Pebbles** (1966) was quickly withdrawn from roadshow release, despite the

Top Left: *Camelot* had plenty of spectacular scenes on the Technicolor and Panavision screen, such as the chivalric one illustrated, but it was a costly flop. However, John Truscott's costumes made from coarse linen and raw silk won an Oscar.

Bottom left: Lancelot (Franco Nero, in armor), King Arthur (Richard Harris, kneeling right) and his wife Guinevere (Vanessa Redgrave, right) in Joshua Logan's $15 million *Camelot* (1967), Lerner and Loewe's musical version of the classic Round Table love triangle.

Right: 'If They Could See Me Now' sings dynamic taxi dancer Shirley MacLaine in former dancer and choreographer Bob Fosse's first film *Sweet Charity* (1969), a rather strident and gaudy version of the hit Broadway musical.

Below: Sammy Davis Jr (center), in a guest spot in *Sweet Charity*, belts out a pseudo-religious rock song entitled 'Rhythm of Life'.

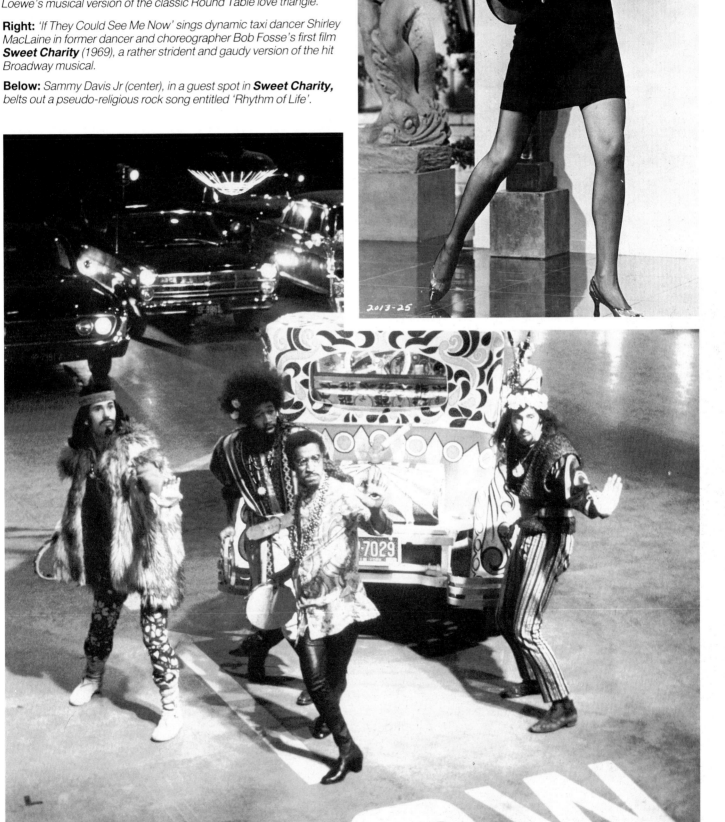

presence of Steve McQueen. It did not do nearly as well ($13.5 million) as the record-breaking actioner **The Dirty Dozen** (1967), with Lee Marvin ($20.3 million). The trouble was that the public expected something special from a blockbuster and when they didn't get it they were inclined to tell their friends not to go and see it, or so the industry thought.

Vision of things to come

MGM did roadshow **2001: A Space Odyssey** (1968) in some engagements, sometimes utilizing those theaters that had been used for Cinerama. The special effects of this sci-fi epic had cost a small fortune, and had been undertaken only because the director, Stanley Kubrick, had an impressive record with critics and young audiences. The former did not much care for **2001**, but the latter did and **2001** was in the long run a huge moneymaker, as to a lesser extent was **Planet of the Apes** (1968). With the exception of Disney's **20,000 Leagues Under the Sea** (1954), these were the first occasions on which Hollywood had allocated large budgets to science-fiction movies, traditionally a cheap genre, although it was not until the Seventies that the sci-fi explosion began.

Still, it was obvious that audience loyalties were shifting. Westerns began to die out — despite the lesser or greater popularity of some memorable ones: **The Magnificent Seven** (1960), with Yul Brynner

Left: *Lee Marvin and Charles Bronson (foreground on floor), two of* **The Dirty Dozen** *(1967), lose their trousers in a tense moment from Robert Aldrich's violent and rugged wartime adventure that spawned dozens of imitations.*

Right: *The grand-daddy of space operas: Stanley Kubrick's* **2001: A Space Odyssey** *(1968) set new standards in special effects.*

Below left: *Set during the California Gold Rush,* **Paint Your Wagon** *(1969) starred Clint Eastwood and Lee Marvin as two prospectors who set up a Mormon menage with the same wife (Jean Seberg).*

Below: *Non-singers Eastwood (left) and Marvin (right) each got to sing in the sluggish musical* **Paint Your Wagon**. *Eastwood warbled 'I Talk To The Trees', and Marvin scored a hit by croaking 'Wandrin' Star'.*

and Steve McQueen; **El Dorado** (1967), with John Wayne and Robert Mitchum; **True Grit** (1969), which brought Wayne an Oscar at last; and **Butch Cassidy and the Sundance Kid** (1969) – these last two in the top ten of their year. Despite that "proof" of the genre's popularity, the success of **True Grit** was thought to be due to Wayne's award and that of **Butch Cassidy** to the buddy-buddy teaming of Paul Newman and Robert Redford, and not really to the reworking of old Western themes. Burt Lancaster had a success with **The Professionals** (1966) but a failure with **The Hallelujah Trail** (1965), underlining the fact that star-appeal was not enough, unless it came with new blood like Clint Eastwood.

There may have been two Western hits in 1969, but there were also several failures, including **The Undefeated**, starring Wayne and Rock Hudson, and **Tell Them Willie Boy Is Here** with Redford, considered to be a hot attraction. Gregory Peck was unable to draw the public with either **The Stalking Moon** or **Mackenna's Gold**, despite good notices for the first and all-star support for the second. Sam Peckinpah's **The Wild Bunch** starred William Holden, Robert

Left: *Despite Rex Harrison's charm as* **Doctor Dolittle** *(1967), and such creatures as Chee-Chee the chimp, Polynesia the parakeet and the Great Pink Sea Snail (all illustrated), the expensive 152-minute musical was a giant turkey.*

Below: *Jack Lemmon (left) and Walter Matthau (right) hilariously at odds in* **The Odd Couple** *(1968), the film version of Neil Simon's hit comedy about two divorced men sharing an apartment.*

Ryan, Edmond O'Brien and Ernest Borgnine, the reviews were fair to good, and much publicity accrued from accusations of excessive violence, but the public still mostly stayed away.

Safety first

Comedies and thrillers were safer box-office bets than Westerns — provided the jokes and the thrills were there. Two versions of Neil Simon's Broadway comedy plays did well — **Barefoot in the Park** (1967), with Redford and Jane Fonda ($9 million); and **The Odd Couple** (1968), with Jack Lemmon and Walter Matthau ($20 million): and two cleverly plotted thrillers, **The Thomas Crown Affair** (1968) and **Bullitt** (1968), scored a double for Steve McQueen. The screen's pre-eminent exponent of the thriller, Alfred Hitchcock, had wowed audiences with **Psycho** (1960) and, to a lesser extent, **The Birds** (1963). But **Torn Curtain** (1966), a Cold War suspenser starring Paul Newman and Julie Andrews, and **Topaz** (1969) perhaps showed him

Above: *Audrey Hepburn made a leap from gamine to cosmopolitan sophisticate in Stanley Donen's flashy Hitchcockian thriller* **Charade** *(1963) opposite suave Cary Grant. It was their only film together, though Grant was offered Professor Higgins in* **My Fair Lady** *(1964).*

Right: *In between playing Mr Tough Guy in Don Siegel's* **Coogan's Bluff** *(1968), Clint Eastwood becomes tender with New York social worker Susan Clark, while remaining impassive and laconic.*

at his least effective.

Failures by other leading directors towards the end of the decade included Elia Kazan with **The Arrangement** (1969), Joseph L. Mankiewicz with **There Was a Crooked Man . . .** (1970), George Stevens with **The Only Game in Town** (1970) and William Wyler with **The Liberation of L.B. Jones** (1970). Between them they had provided the American cinema with some of its greatest films; now they all walked away from it.

The stars of the Stevens film were Warren Beatty and Elizabeth Taylor, supposedly hot properties although Taylor, still drawing a large salary, was embarking on a long run of flops, as was her husband Richard Burton. In fact, one of the reasons for the huge losses sustained by the Hollywood studios in 1969-70 was due to the

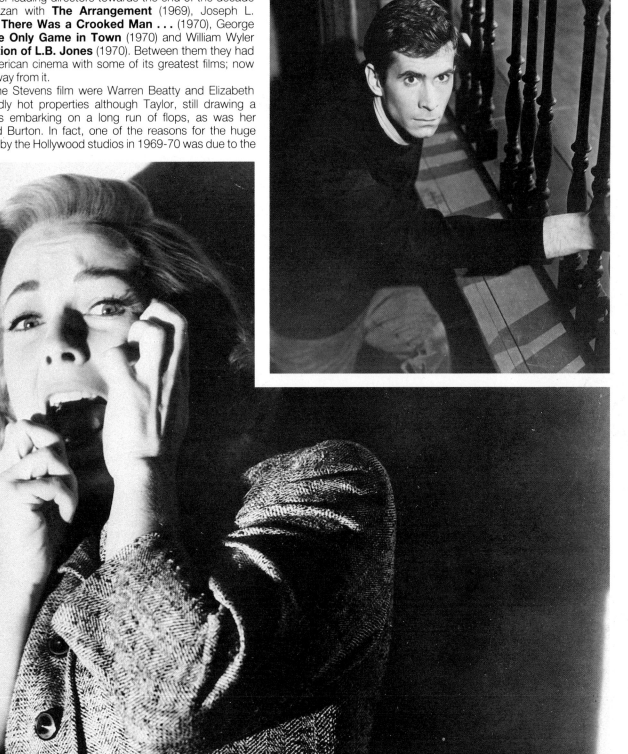

Left: *Rod Taylor, already pretty pecked, faces another of his feathered enemies in Alfred Hitchcock's ornithophobic **The Birds** (1963), a superb transformation of the mundane into the nightmarish.*

Above: *After Janet Leigh is disposed of in a celebrated, bloody manner in the shower in Alfred Hitchcock's first real horror movie*

*Psycho (1960), another 'cool blonde' Vera Miles (illustrated) appears to search for her missing sister. The same film starred Anthony Perkins **(top)** in his memorable role as the maniac motel keeper Norman Bates. Just as Norman identified with this dead mother, so Perkins has always been identified with the character he created.*

colossal fees they were paying performers who were no longer box-office draws.

There were 13 names in the box-office top-ten lists of 1960 and 1961, and only John Wayne and Jack Lemmon survived to the top tens of 1969 and 1970. Of the others, Cary Grant had retired; Doris Day had gone into television after some movie failures; Sandra Dee had disappeared after some flops; audiences were no longer interested in Rock Hudson, Frank Sinatra, William Holden or Elvis Presley; Debbie Reynolds was to make no more films; and Jerry Lewis and Elizabeth Taylor were both box-office liabilities. Apart from Wayne and Lemmon, the names in the 1969 and 1970 top tens are Paul Newman, Dustin Hoffman, Steve McQueen, Clint Eastwood,

Lee Marvin, Sidney Poitier, Elliott Gould, Barbra Streisand, Katharine Hepburn and Walter Matthau. A couple of years later, only half of these would still be box-office attractions. In other words, for the first time in Hollywood's history stars no longer guaranteed success.

These years saw some surprising box-office hits. They included Roman Polanski's **Rosemary's Baby** (1968), a thriller involving

Left and above: *Julie Andrews trying bravely to be convincing as Gertrude Lawrence in* **Star!** *(1968), an old-hat biopic that cost $12 million. After its failure on first release, it was re-released under the title* **Those Were the Happy Days**. *It flopped again.*

Left: *Peter O'Toole and Katharine Hepburn as Henry II and Eleanor of Aquitaine in* **The Lion in Winter** *(1968), a tragi-comic depiction of 12th century power politics.*

Below: *Naked Ape Charlton Heston embraces lady ape (Kim Hunter somewhere under John Chambers' effective make-up) in* **Planet Of The Apes** *(1968), the first of a string of science fiction monkey tales.*

diabolism with Mia Farrow and John Cassavetes; **The Fox** (1968), a lesbian-oriented tale, from a story by D.H. Lawrence, with Sandy Dennis, Ann Heywood and Keir Dullea; **I Am Curious — Yellow**, an explicit Swedish sex movie; **The Lion in Winter** (1968), a historical charade with Peter O'Toole and Katharine Hepburn; **M*A*S*H** (1970), a bloody "anything goes" comedy set in a US army field hospital in Korea and starring Elliott Gould and Donald Sutherland;

Above: *Freshly divorced from Frank Sinatra, Mia Farrow scored her first major screen success with **Rosemary's Baby** (1968), a lurid adaptation of Ira Levin's novel about Satanic practices in New York.*

Left: *Jane Fonda in the title role of **Cat Ballou** (1965), a school marm in the Wild West who hires a gunfighter to get the man who shot her father. In the same year, Fonda married French director Roger Vadim, who tried to make her into another Bardot.*

and **Woodstock** (1970), a documentary record of the huge rock festival in upstate New York which signified the apogee of hippiedom.

The flops were many and varied, and there is little point in listing them, since some failed so completely that they have no revival value — even on late-night television. The great Hollywood studios had begun to change hands during the Sixties, being either swallowed up by conglomerates or absorbed by new, ambitious companies with show-business interests. After some doubts, they retained their famous old names, so that in the 1969-70 period we can see Paramount announcing a loss of $22 million, MGM $35 million, United Artists $50 million, Warner Bros. $59 million and 20th Century-Fox over $100 million. Columbia waited a couple of years before noting a write-off of $82 million (along with Universal, it was the only studio not to acquire new owners — and, indeed, Universal was very well managed by MCA).

Above: *Oversized leprechaun Tommy Steele and Irish immigrant Petula Clark in* **Finian's Rainbow** *(1968), set in a mythical Mississippi. This indigestible musical blend of blarney and social comment was the second movie directed by Francis Ford Coppola, a far cry from his* **Godfather** *pictures.*

Right: *Lee Marvin (right) and Burt Lancaster (left) as two mercenaries hired by a millionaire to bring back his wife Claudia Cardinale, kidnapped by a Mexican bandit in* **The Professionals** *(1966), Richard Brooks' ochre-colored Western.*

The industry reeled, not knowing where to turn. The public could not be relied upon for clues. Variously during the Sixties it wanted nuns, kids and songs; pornography; old-fashioned Disney fun; James Bond; hippies on a drug trip; blood and jokes in an operating theater; Shakespeare; spaceships hurtling through the universe; devils; and parents debating whether their daughter should marry a black man. The public had never signaled in the past that it wanted to see such films, and if the studios now offered anything similar they were just as likely to be greeted by empty theaters, as occurred with the countless attempts to recapture the audiences of **Easy Rider**. Formula movies seemed as moribund as the studio system and the star system, except that in 1970 Universal presented **Airport**, a portmanteau

Right and below: *The popular tandem of Paul Newman (right in main picture) and Robert Redford as* **Butch Cassidy and the Sundance Kid** *(1969), legendary outlaws who finished their days in the dusty towns of Bolivia.*

You never met a pair like Butch and The Kid

They're Taking Trains...
They're Taking Banks
And They're Taking
One Piece Of Baggage!

20th Century-Fox presents

PAUL NEWMAN
ROBERT REDFORD
KATHARINE ROSS

BUTCH CASSIDY AND THE SUNDANCE KID

Co-Starring STROTHER MARTIN, JEFF COREY, HENRY JONES.

A George Roy Hill–Paul Monash Production Directed by GEORGE ROY HILL Written by WILLIAM GOLDMAN
Executive Producer PAUL MONASH Produced by JOHN FOREMAN A NEWMAN-FOREMAN Presentation PANAVISION® COLOUR BY DE LUXE
Music Composed and Conducted by BURT BACHARACH

Left: Sam Peckinpah's gory horse opera **The Wild Bunch** (1969) earned a reputation for gratuitous violence but is now seen as one of his best films. William Holden and Ernest Borgnine starred. Angel (Jaime Sanchez) has his throat cut by the renegade 'General'.

Right: Lee Marvin as the drunken, has-been gunfighter in Elliott Silverstein's spoof Western **Cat Ballou** (1965). Marvin won the best actor Oscar for the double role as the dipso and the meanest varmint in the West.

Left: *George C. Scott as **Patton** (1969), the controversial 'blood and guts' American World War II general. Scott himself proved to be as controversial by becoming the first actor ever to refuse an Oscar.*

Below: *Although most of **Bird Man of Alcatraz** (1962) takes place in a prison cell, the intensity of John Frankenheimer's direction and Burt Lancaster's mesmeric performance brilliantly sustain it over 2½ hours.*

disaster movie based on a formula going back to the Thirties at least, and it was so successful that it called for three sequels, equally old-fashioned and welcomed, if decreasingly, by moviegoers.

Richard Zanuck, the son of Fox's Darryl F. Zanuck and already an experienced producer in his own right, said at this time: "The rule-book has been thrown away. Today almost anything goes. Frankly, I go on what pleases me personally because I just can't tell what pleases the audience anymore."

Easy Rider *(1969) was a 'sleeper' whose combination of drugs, rock music, violence and motor bikes caught the imagination of the young. Illustrated are Dennis Hopper (left, the film's director), Peter Fonda (foreground, the producer), and Jack Nicholson (right).*

Top left: *Nice locations, shame about the plot. Elvis Presley in his salad days in* **Blue Hawaii** *(1961).*

Bottom left: *Not one of The Duke's greatest roles, but John Wayne won a sentimental Oscar for his role as the boozing, one-eyed marshal in* **True Grit** *(1969).*

Below: *Steve McQueen in one of his most memorable roles as the rebel POW in* **The Great Escape** *(1963). McQueen pulled off all his motorcycle stunts himself.*

Top left: *Clint Eastwood as a deputy sheriff from Arizona in New York in* **Coogan's Bluff** *(1968), 'interviews' a suspect in his own subtle way. The film was Eastwood's first collaboration with director Don Siegel with whom he made four others including* **Dirty Harry** *(1971).*

Bottom left: *Norman Jewison's* **In The Heat Of The Night** *(1967) was an effective attack on racial prejudice in the form of a crime thriller, Sidney Poitier (standing left), black homicide expert, confronts bigoted redneck cop Rod Steiger (right).*

Below: *Frank Sinatra as* **The Detective** *(1968), a hard-bitten cop investigating the murder of a homosexual. Explicit for its time, the movie now seems reactionary, and no less nasty.*

Back to the future?

Pleasing the audience in 1968 was another revival of **Gone With the Wind**. The decade of blockbusters produced a desperate search for another almighty hit — unexpectedly found in **The Sound of Music**. That proved a false dawn, certifiably a throwback when the "family" entertainments that followed it all flopped. Cinemas continued to close, so that censorship was relaxed in an attempt to persuade people to emerge from their homes to see the sort of product not shown on the television screen, but that was no long-term solution. From 1969 to 1970 Hollywood was fighting for its survival.

Which is where we came in, except that in 1960 the film industry refused to see how desperate the struggle would be. Yet the battle for survival was won — excepting one casualty of the Fifties, RKO, all

the major studios still existed (and still do). Furthermore the decade had produced a wide range of enduring movies — from **The Misfits** to **Coogan's Bluff** (1968), from **The Magnificent Seven** to **Midnight Cowboy**, from **The Hustler** (1961) to **True Grit**, from **The Apartment** to **Easy Rider**. Come to think of it, there aren't many films of the Seventies or Eighties that you'd swop for these, or **2001: A Space Odyssey**, **Psycho**, **How to Succeed in Business Without Really Trying** (1967), **The Deadly Affair** (1967), **Cat Ballou** (1965), **Charade** (1963), **Dr Strangelove**, **The Hill** (1965), **One, Two, Three** (1961). And there's hardly a blockbuster among them.

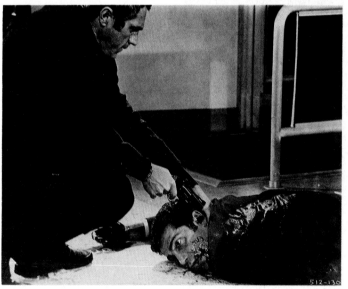

Above: *Steve McQueen (left) as the San Francisco cop checks that the dead gangster (Felice Orlandi) really is dead this time in* **Bullitt** *(1968), the movie with the car chase to end all car chases.*

Top: ***The Pawnbroker*** *(Rod Steiger) is confronted, but not tempted, by a prostitute (Thelma Oliver) about to bare her breasts in an epoch-making scene from Sidney Lumet's 1965 version of Edward Lewis Wallant's novel.*

Left: *Julie Andrews plays an uncharacteristic role as a German spy in* **Darling Lili** *(1970), an eccentric World War One espionage caper also rejoicing in the sub-title of* **Where Were You the Night I Shot Down Baron von Richthofen?**

PICTURE CREDITS